Meet Me
in the Meadow

Finding God in the Wildflowers

Deborah Hedstrom-Page
Illustrations by Kevin Ingram

Revell
Grand Rapids, Michigan

Published by Fleming H. Revell
a division of Baker Publishing Group
P.O. Box 6287, Grand Rapids, MI 49516-6287

Printed in the United States of America

Library of Congress Cataloging-in-Publication Data
Hedstrom-Page, Deborah, 1951-
    Meet me in the meadow : finding God in the wildflowers / Deborah Hed-
strom-Page ; illustrations by Kevin Ingram
        p.   cm.
    Includes bibliographical references.
    ISBN 0-8007-5946-X (pbk.)
    1. Flowers—Religious aspects—Christianity. 2. Wild flowers. 3. Wild-
flowers—Miscellanea. I. Title.
    BV168.F56H43 2005
    242—dc22   2004021710

The information in this book is not medical or health advice. Readers are reminded
to use extreme caution in properly identifying the wildflowers discussed, as many
wild plants have toxic parts or can cause allergic reactions. Check with a medical
or health care professional before using any wild plant medicinally, nutritionally,
or for health and other reasons. The reader assumes all risks for performing the
treatments and following the nutritional ideas in *Meet Me in the Meadow*.

Interior design by Brian Brunsting

Meet Me *in the* Meadow

To Arthur John Hedstrom, my first husband, who died of cancer at the age of thirty-five and who gave me my first wildflower book. It began the expansion of my "Oh, that's so pretty" to the added knowledge and many thoughts used in this book.

Contents

Fields of Wonder: *Your Welcome
into the Wild*   9

To see a world in a grain of sand,
And a heaven in a wild flower,
Hold infinity in the palm of your hand,
An eternity in an hour.

William Blake

Fields of Wonder

Your Welcome into the Wild

The earth brought forth vegetation, plants yielding seed
after their kind, and trees bearing fruit with seed in them,
after their kind; and God saw that it was good.

Genesis 1:12 NASB

The frozen dirt still crunched beneath my feet when
I spotted the first wildflower at our new country
home. Backdropped by late winter's dry pine needles and
decomposed fall leaves, the trillium stood out like a dollop
of whipped cream on brown carpet.

A few days later, I saw a yellow violet and then a wild iris.
Having been a town girl all my life, I was fascinated by each
one. Daily, I began to watch for new beauties that broke
through the soil and reached for the sun.

Their details amazed me—perfectly matched petals in an
endless blend of color, shape, size, and number. There were

bells and stars, doves and pinwheels. Each one made me say, "Wow, God. Incredible. So perfect, so unique."

I could picture the Lord at creation. I imagined him as a glassblower or cabinetmaker carefully designing each flower, drawing from his eternity of beauty, purity, and knowledge—divine resources beyond my comprehension.

The intimate connection to my God added to each wild-flower's allure. I wanted to know their names. What was the stately, three-petaled one called, or the orange one with leopard spots?

My first wildflower book identified the trillium and tiger lily, but that knowledge wasn't enough. Soon trips became flower hunts, and a tripod and close-up lenses let me bring each flower home in photos. And my single book became a library collection. I learned how Native Americans, early settlers, and other people used these wild plants as flours, decongestants, hair conditioners, and more. I found out why some can grow without sunlight and why others grow in the shallows of lakes and ponds.

As I learned, my new knowledge began slipping into my times with God. I'd be reading about him never leaving me or forsaking me and suddenly remember the tiny blue forget-me-nots I'd found along the river where we'd camped the previous summer (Heb. 13:5). Or I'd be registering the switch from ashes to beauty in Isaiah and a mental picture would come to mind of the thousands of fireweed spires I'd seen transform a roadside burn into a field of bright pink (61:3). And when I read of lilies outdressing even Solomon, I knew exactly what Christ meant (Matt. 6:28–29).

My studies, imaginings, prayers, and delight led me to a profound truth about these beautiful creations. If given more than an "Ahh, that's pretty" look, they provide a glimpse of God. They don't preach sermons, shout praises, or quote

Scripture. But the Lord designed their patterns. He colored their petals and leaves. He gave them useful qualities. And he breathed life into their delicate being.

Because God played this intimate role in each wildflower's creation, their features give insight to him. My hope is that you too can find those riches—that as you learn about each flower's attributes, you'll register parallel Scripture verses and discover ways that each petaled beauty reveals an attribute of God's character and your own.

Never again will you view in the same way the annual spring splashes of color along roadsides, in vacant lots, and in your own backyard. When you see one of the many wildflowers in this book, you'll remember how it reflects its Creator, and you'll see a new glimpse of God.

Anemone

1

Anemone

Anemone Deltoide[1]

*A*lthough an anemone's blossom looks like every child's first drawings of a flower, it actually has no petals. Instead, its sepals[2] play the part. Their delicate thinness, oval shape, and white color mimic petals to perfection. Often they even have blue or fuchsia veins, pin-striping the blooms and leaving a bluish or pinkish blush.

This common-looking but unusual wild plant is also called "wind flower." Some people credit its second name to the blossom's thin stem and petals that quake in the slightest breeze. But the name actually came from how its seeds spread. Like many other wildflowers, anemones produce plumy seeds that ride the wind in scattered directions.

Beyond its looks and seeds, the anemone produces a powerful irritant drug and should never be eaten as a cooked green or in salads.

My Wonderings . . .

For since the creation of the world God's invisible qualities—
his eternal power and divine nature—have been clearly seen,
being understood from what has been made.

Romans 1:20

The first time I found an anemone in the woods by my house,
I recognized it. Though I'd never actually seen the flower before and didn't know its name, I'd drawn it a hundred times
as a child. With crayons and pencils I sketched its simple
five-petal blossom from the memory of flowers in gardens,
pictures in books, and what I'd seen at the beach.

I grew up just a few miles from a coastline with lots of
seashells. While still in elementary school, I found my first
whole sand dollar. On its top, I saw an etched five-petaled
flower just like the ones in gardens and books.

How could a flower get drawn on the hard shell? Of course,
only God could do it. In that moment, everything I'd learned
about him in Sunday school became true. God was real and
capable of anything. He had not only made this flower but
reached under the ocean and etched into a hard shell something beautiful.

Remembering my first real awareness of God made me take
another look at the anemone I found in the woods. I smiled.
God was still using flowers to help me know him.

You can find the anemone May through July in temperate subarctic climates. Look for mostly white blooms that can range in color from red to purple.

Aftereffects

Relish the wisdom of a child. Encourage a child in your life to draw some flowers. Then go to your garden or a field of wildflowers to compare the artwork to the real thing. Ask who "drew" the real flowers. Let the discussion take its natural course. Muse together on God's handiwork.

Dry some blooms. Preserve a remembrance from this time together! Since anemone petals are fragile and moist, dry them with a compound of borax and sand. (You can also use silica gel, available at most florist shops, and follow the label instructions.) Mix three parts borax with two parts dry, silver "hobby" sand.

Spread several flowers faceup on a bed of the borax-sand mix in a shallow, airtight, plastic or glass container. Spoon more mix on top, until you've completely covered the flowers with another two inches. Seal the container and don't disturb it for six to eight days.

To remove the delicate blossoms, carefully shake or brush off the sand mix with a soft artist's paintbrush. Leaving flowers too long makes them very fragile, so remove flowers as soon as you determine they're dry enough.

2

Bear Grass

Xerophyllum Tenax

*T*he small white blossoms of bear grass, also called elk grass, cover the large cone-shaped ball that sits on its single stout stalk. A thick clump of grasslike leaves surrounds its base.

Its common names come from the fact that bear and elk like to munch on this native flower's tender basal greenery. Native American tribes dug a bit deeper, roasting and eating its fibrous root,[3] but they found even more value in the wildflower's long, narrow leaves.

Tribal women dried and bleached the tough blades, even coloring some with plant dyes. Then they wove the treated leaves into baskets, hats, clothing, and even watertight cooking pots. The quality of these items caused this plant's foliage to be prized among the tribes, and they often used it in trading and bartering.

My Wonderings . . .

> But we have this treasure in earthen vessels, that the excellence of the power may be of God and not of us.
>
> 2 Corinthians 4:7 NKJV

In these days of stainless steel and "unbreakable" ceramics, reed containers are used only for decoration. Looking at their crisscrossed strips, I can't imagine using them for meat or chopped vegetables. Remnants would stick in their cracks. Bacteria and germs would multiply in the fibers. The vessel would discolor—and never have a lifetime warranty.

Yet God uses vessels created from the earth—you . . . me. He knows I am only dust but still entrusts me with the knowledge and sharing of his Son.

Recently I sought to keep that trust by speaking at a women's retreat while also teaching at a Christian college. The busy schedule and emotional drain of both brought on an illness. Frustrated and discouraged, I told God, "Look at me. I can't even handle using the gifts you gave me."

"You're right," he answered. "As dust, you're frail . . . but I still used you."

Thinking back to the women at the retreat, I remembered what one told me. "I want to fall in love with God like you have." Another said, "You've encouraged me to go home and keep loving my wayward daughter."

And then I thought of a student who had come to my office. "I want to be a writer," she told me. "Like you, I want to use words to share God."

I felt amazed. Had God used me, frail as I was, to help these women?

"Yes, Lord. You did."

Woven Wonders

Remember the simple under-over-under weave required on childhood pot-holder looms? Try doing that same easy weave with split bear grass leaves (which can be one-foot to two-and-a-half-feet long) or—closer to home—with split iris leaves.

Gather the leaves and lay them flat on a dry surface to cure in the sun. (Be careful as you can slice your fingers on the leaves.) To flatten the leaves completely, lay them between two pieces of weighted plywood or cutting boards. Now put several pieces of grass side by side onto the sticky side of some tape. Add a strip of tape on top to "seal" the width. Take the end strand from one side and weave it in and out, across the grass. When you reach the other side, bend the strand over and weave it back the other way. To add length to a strand, just add a new leaf on top of the old and keep going. Keep the weave tight against the last row for a strong result.

Join your finished weaving into a cone by sewing the two sides together with wire, raffia, or more grass.

Your Wanderings . . .

You can't miss the stately, tall bear grass in early summer, when, as a member of the lily family, its blooms are a delicacy for deer, elk, and wild sheep or mountain goats. Bears not only dine on the grass (thus its name), but they also pluck it to make thick mats and nests in their winter beds. In mountain-ous areas, through August, bear grass can spread so profusely that sunny clearings and open slopes appear peppered with pale flickering candles, which are really just the yellowish white flowers in full bloom.

Beckstrau

3

Bedstraw

Galium Aparine

$\mathcal{B}$edstraw's tiny white blossoms barely reach the eighth-inch mark on a ruler. Most people wouldn't even notice the five-petaled blooms if the plant didn't cling to their clothes. Its clinging quality comes from thousands of tiny hooked hairs that cover the wildflower's square-stemmed vine and swirls of quadruple leaves.

Despite the sticky tendencies, bedstraw's abundant vines and tiny blooms have had a variety of uses. Historically, people have roasted its seeds as a coffee substitute, boiled its roots for a dye, and steeped its leaves for medicinal tea, hair tonic, and body perfume.

But another use led to its common name. Medieval and pioneer women stuffed the dried plant into mattresses because the vines, leaves, and blooms provided good cushioning with a pleasant smell.

My Wonderings . . .

Do not despise this small beginning, for the eyes of the
Lord rejoice to see the work begin.

Zechariah 4:10 TLB

I like the sense of satisfaction that comes from finishing a big
job. When I stand back and look at the garage after painting
it or when I push the print button on a book manuscript, I
feel great. I want to celebrate—do a little dance, shout "Yes!"
or eat chocolate.

Yet every big accomplishment gets finished by completing
dozens of little ones—a brushstroke here, just a sentence
there.

No wonder God told Zechariah not to despise the small
steps of progress made in rebuilding the temple after the
Israelites came home from their Babylonian captivity.

Progress in our lives happens the same way. We want to
see the "big" change—the problem fixed, the situation re-
solved, the flawed character transformed. It's easy, then, to
be unimpressed with a modest good deed or single kind word.
And yet . . .

Many modest deeds can fix a problem, and a pattern of
kind words can transform a person's character. Great end
results should cause celebration. But so should small, simple
steps. God even cheered to see a plumb line* in the hand of
Israel's leader.

This "despise not the little things" quality of God causes me
to think, *No wonder he made tiny, pretty flowers like bedstraw,
and not just tall, majestic ones.*

*A weighted line that helps determine if something is straight up and down.

Look for bedstraw blooms April through September when the small white or greenish white flowers grow on short branches in leaf axles or clusters and whorls.

Sachet This Way

We no longer use home-stuffed mattresses, but a fragrant sachet makes a pleasant addition to a drawer or closet. Create your own.[4] Collect bunches of bedstraw flowers and hang them upside down in clusters, tied together at the stem, in a moisture-free place. Once the plants are dry, separate them. You may want to chop them (but not too fine) to stuff into your sachet. The natural pleasant scent, which is similar to honey or vanilla, can be supplemented with commercial scent of essential oils.

Bedstraw also yields several fabric dyes (for towels, tablecloths, and yarn). Dig up the roots in fall. Use them fresh or wash and dry them for later use. Boil four to six ounces of fresh or dried bedstraw roots in one gallon of water for about two hours for a yellow dye. For red dye, add alum to the boiling roots, or add iron for a plum color.

4

Bitterroot

Lewisia Rediviva

The succulent leaves and showy, water lily–like flowers of bitterroot don't seem to belong in the arid, rocky ground where this wildflower grows in abundance. But the blossom's light pink to rose petals love the sun, only unfurling under conditions bright and hot.

Beneath this low-growing wildflower lies a nutritious carrot-shaped root. Native Americans harvested it in the spring when its bitter skin could be rubbed off. Then they boiled or baked the exposed white tuber[5] to expunge the last of the bitter taste.

Whether cooked immediately or dried for winter use, bitterroot made a valuable food staple. Tribes considered a sack full of the roots an equal exchange for a horse.

Lewis and Clark, however, weren't as enthralled with the bland-tasting root, even though at one point in their expedition west, over the Rockies, it saved their lives.

My Wonderings . . .

That the genuineness of your faith, *being* much more precious than gold that perishes, though it is tested by fire, may be found to praise, honor, and glory at the revelation of Jesus Christ.

1 Peter 1:7 NKJV

God is into "fire" metaphors. In the Bible, if he's not purifying gold, he's refining silver. So it really shouldn't surprise us that many of the plants he created require a fire's heat before they can be useful.

It doesn't take a theologian to figure out how all these flaming metaphors apply to our lives. Yet when circumstances heat up our day, knowing our character will be refined isn't enough. We need a "God moment" to grasp the hope of a purified, shiny inner self.

Once when feeling scorched, I started berating God.

When I finished, he asked only one thing. "What if I wasn't here?"

"Oh no!" In the instant it took to speak those words, I realized that rebuffing God would not take away life's fiery hurts. With or without him, things will still heat up. I must choose. I can go through them alone, or I can go through them with the One who offers the hope of pure and shiny results.

Your Wanderings . . .

Also called "rockrose," bitterroot sprouts from sagebrush-covered steppes, the hidden crevices of rocky ridges, and gravel river bars once its delicate blooms open in early summer. Until the plant blooms, though, it can go unnoticed, as

Picture This

Record for yourself the hearty pluck and strength-giving properties of the bitterroot, looking at how its appearance changes over the course of a single day. (Outdoor enthusiasts can attest that bitterroot will survive in very arid conditions and has even grown after being dug up, allowed to dry, and then replanted.)

Make a montage of pictures that capture bitterroot's strength. Photograph a bitterroot plant in early fall, when its narrow leaves grow from one to four inches. Photograph the plant again in winter and notice how the leaves may still be green. In late spring, photograph the bitterroot's emerging buds and blooms. Watch and record with your camera how the buds open a bright fuchsia color that within hours will fade to light pink. Several hours after blossoming, the bloom dies and turns to a transparent white. Frame the results for your home or a friend's, or use them on a greeting card for encouragement.

it grows low to the ground and its leaves are not notable like the blooms. As the Montana state flower, bitterroot can only be found north and south of this region. It's worth looking for this plant when traveling through the area in June. Overcast days with in-and-out sunshine make for the best displays. Patches of bitterroot will bloom each time the sun appears and close when the sun slips behind a cloud.

5

Bleeding Heart

Dicentra Formosa

ernlike leaves backdrop this wildflower's dangling rows of magenta hearts. Its beauty caused settlers to transplant it near doors and walkways, but Native Americans found more practical uses. One Northwest tribe chewed the roots to help toothaches, while others soaked the crushed greenery in water for a child's hair-growth shampoo.

Whether used practically or decoratively, bleeding heart is easy to spot. Two sets of oddly shaped petals create the heart appearance that earned the flower half its name. The other half came from the pierced look it gets when it goes to seed. Out of the bottom of the "heart," a spike appears.

Eventually the bloom shrivels as the spike grows long and turns into a pod. Though these pods contain poisonous alkaloids, they also hold seeds for next spring's display of dangling hearts.

My Wonderings . . .

> But He was pierced through for our transgressions,
> He was crushed for our iniquities;
> The chastening for our well-being *fell* upon Him,
> And by His scourging we are healed.

Isaiah 53:5 NASB

For years God's biblical requirement of shed blood to cover sin bothered my mother. She willingly accepted the eternal life that Christ's death and resurrection provided, but her nurse's training created uneasiness with God's insistence that Christ shed his blood. More than most people, she knew that blood gave life; blood did not take it.

Living out this strong awareness, she donated her rare Rh-negative blood regularly.

In his patient, loving way, God gradually helped my mom come to grips with her unease. Every time she went to the bloodmobile, wasn't she "spilling blood" to give life? And how can the essence of life not be connected to saving life?

These questions and the imprint of God on my mom's heart led her to a deep appreciation of Christ's blood sacrifice. What once was paradox became real, absolute truth: giving life meant getting it. Shedding blood produced life.

Your Wanderings . . .

Look for bleeding hearts March through July in damp, shaded places or wetter climates and open woods. You'll also find the wildflower in many gardens, since it's been domesticated for more than a century; a variety of hybrid colors and sizes can be bought at any nursery.[6] In fact, the bleeding heart

Pressed Hearts

Bleeding hearts make the perfect pressed flowers. Not only are the blooms fun to pick (especially with children present) and playful to wear as "earrings" or to weave into the hair as a dancing heart tiara, but they also preserve well.

Pick blooms early in the morning and place them on a paper towel to dry from the dew. This will take a few hours. Then tuck the blooms between sheets of wax paper and the pages of a thick dictionary, Bible, or even the phone book.

After a few weeks you'll find the blooms transformed into perfectly flat, papery little hearts. Dry these on a paper towel a few weeks more before gluing on greeting cards or using in craft projects like bookmark making.

is a garden favorite of poets, hummingbirds, and children who dissect the blooms to reveal what appears as a lady in a bathtub or a man riding in a gondola.

6

Blue Flag

Iris Missouriensis

The unique bloom of a blue flag combines colorful upward-curved petals with downward-curved sepals. Contrasting colored centers and dark vein patterns add to the bloom's distinctive "iris" look.

Though the blue flag variety hails from the Midwest, its many family members bring the same recognizable flower to fields throughout the United States. Some stand tall, while others grow close to the ground. Some favor blue and purple hues, while others opt for yellow or white. But their blossoms are unmistakably iris.

In addition to having unique colors and sizes, this wild-flower family also boasts a variety of uses. Some go into sweet-smelling sachets, while others are boiled into a poison that Native Americans used to dip their arrow tips. Another variety even has tough leaf fibers that make great twine and cords.

My Wonderings . . .

And it was so. . . . And God saw that it was good.

Genesis 1:11–12

Recently I reread the creation account in the first chapter of Genesis. Though I'd been through the story dozens of times, the phrase "and God saw that it was good" stuck out more than usual. I even noted in my journal that it appeared five times with a sixth "very good" to top it off.

Thinking about what I'd recorded, I realized the obvious— God sought to make something good when he created the earth. He didn't work haphazardly or by whim but had a plan. Each time he finished an aspect of creation, he stepped back, examined it, felt pleasure, and declared it well done. I know that "step back" act in my writing. When I finish something, I reread the text to evaluate my effort. But unlike God, I don't always think it's good.

A wildflower like blue flag lets me see why God declared his creation to be of such high quality. It has an artist's striking beauty and an inventor's variety of helpful uses. God designed it well, from the depths of its roots to the peak of its petals—and this was only one of hundreds of plants and trees.

Your Wanderings . . .

Look for blue flag June through July in marshy areas, wet meadows, and wooded edges, where the soil is sandy or a moist loam. Imagine the joy American settlers felt, claiming a bit of royalty in the wild as they named this wildflower be-

Domestic irises are easily grown and readily purchased as cut flowers. Make a bouquet for your church, whether it be simply placed in a vase or artfully arranged. The irises' beauty alone can remind fellow worshipers that God is good. Think on this and on this poem by Henry Wadsworth Longfellow as you arrange the flowers—and make the act a living prayer:

Beautiful lily, dwelling by still rivers,
Or solitary mere,
Or where the sluggish meadow-brook delivers
Its waters to the weir! . . .
The wind blows, and uplifts thy drooping banner,
And round thee throng and run
The rushes, the green yeoman of thy manor,
The outlaws of the sun. . . .
O flower-de-luce, bloom on, and let the river
Linger to kiss thy feet!
O flower of song, bloom on, and make forever
The world more fair and sweet.

cause of its close resemblance to a common European species, the yellow flag, which was the model for the fleur-de-lis—the emblem of French royalty.

7

Bull Thistle

Cirsium Vulgare

*T*he bull thistle's bloom looks like a dense tuft, reminiscent of an old-time shaving brush used to lather a man's face before applying his straight razor. However, most people don't think about the bloom long enough to make the brush comparison. They're too busy avoiding the prickly plant as the pink to lavender bull thistle spouts wicked-looking spines on its leaves and three-foot-high stalk.

Bull thistle, a bold, aggressive, takeover wildflower from Eurasia, has been labeled a "noxious weed" by government land agencies. Though butterflies enjoy its blooms and some birds thrive on its seeds, this plant's thorny exterior sets up barriers to both animals and humans. And after blooming, its lavender tuft becomes a cloud of feathery seeds that spread with the whim of the wind. Where one bull thistle takes root, a half acre of lavender heads can appear the next year.

My Wonderings . . .

> Still others, like seed sown among thorns, hear the word;
> but the worries of this life, the deceitfulness of wealth and
> the desires for other things come in and choke the word,
> making it unfruitful.
>
> Mark 4:18–19

Worry can get a choke hold on me that devastates. It cuts off all thoughts but those focused on the object of my mental wrestling. It blocks me from writing, reading, sleeping, and a dozen other healthy activities.

I've always wanted to find a formula for breaking the vise grip of my worries. For a long time I thought the answer rested in prayer or Bible reading. But even those got stifled by my fretfulness. My godly petitions became cracked records of "God, please fix it." And every verse of Scripture seemed to apply to my anxiety.

No instant fixes, even spiritual ones, force open worry's gripping fingers. Somehow God's peace comes as uniquely as each of my problems. Sometimes he uses the practical—a physical workout, a listening friend, or one who prays for me. At other times, he finally gets me beyond verses that apply to the problem to one that applies to peace. Or after a dozen tearful "fix it" prayers, an exhausted quiet moment allows his Spirit to speak the words I need.

No matter how worry's grip is finally broken, I always look back and see God.

Your Wanderings . . .

Part of the aster family, bull thistles bloom June through September in dry fields and along roadsides. Bees love the pink and magenta blooms, and birds often hide in the silver-gray foliage, but deer and other creatures are wisely wary of the notoriously prickly bull thistle.

In a Thistle

If you spot bull thistles on your property, it's recommended that you take steps to stop them from spreading. First wear protective gloves to handle this pincushion-like plant, then cut off the stalk at ground level before it blooms. If their heads do turn lavender, put the thistle blooms in a bag and burn them.

In spite of this wildflower's negative press, it does make an unusual addition to dried floral arrangements. When the purple tuft disappears and the plant dries to a strawlike color, the old flower head looks like a pretty star. When cutting and arranging these natural starbursts, wear protective gloves.

8

Chicory

Cichorium Intybus

*S*ky blue petals shaped like rays bring fresh beauty to chicory's dandelion-type flower. Up to a dozen blooms soften and decorate each plant's irregular branches. Long, narrow leaves edged with "teeth" surround its base. Below the ground an extended taproot supports the entire wildflower.

The conspicuous blue blooms earned the plant a second name, "blue sailors," for the legend that a young woman was transformed into the blue flower to haunt waysides in search of a lost love who vanished at sea. But it's the plant's nutritious basal leaves and root that led early Europeans to cultivate chicory as a crop.

Various parts of the plant (leaves, blooms, stem, and roots) can be sliced, roasted, and ground. The roots especially make a great hot drink or addition to coffee. These qualities led immigrants to bring the plant to America.

Beekeepers also find chicory desirable. The plant has a unique timer that opens the flowers at 7:00 a.m. and closes them at noon. Bees go to the blooms only during those hours, and the result is exceptional honey.

My Wonderings . . .

> How sweet are your words to my taste,
> sweeter than honey to my mouth!
> I gain understanding from your precepts.

Psalm 119:103–4

Early in my life with God, the Bible seemed more of a duty and source of guilt than sweet honey. I dutifully tried to read it, but when my resolve floundered, guilt came. Only after someone showed me that the Bible was God's love letter did I find its honey quality.

Not a word in the text changed, but the way I came to it did. I opened its pages with expectation and a longing to see God's love for me. When I'd catch a glimpse of his heart or discover a new insight, it felt incredible. Almighty God had spoken to me.

Once after my first husband died and I hungered to feel love again, God whispered to me, as he had to Daniel, "You are my beloved."

Another time when I was single parenting four adolescents and my life was reduced to constant chauffeuring and cooking, he pointed out to me, as he had Jeremiah point out to the captive Israelites in Babylon, "I know the plans I have for you."

And then there was the time when God didn't "fix" a heartache in my life. Instead, he showed me his orchestration of events in Mary's life so that she had continued encouragement when others learned of her seeming illegitimate pregnancy.

Each time, I left God's Word with a divine sweetness that far surpassed a wildflower's honey.

Many people enjoy chicory coffee. Gather roots from the plant. Peel and slice each one, placing the pieces on a shallow pan in a 300-degree oven. Roast slowly until they are hard and can be ground. After they have cooled, grind them and mix one part chicory to one part coffee beans to impart a nutty, slightly bitter taste and darker color.

Another treat to serve with chicory coffee is Chicory and Caerphilly Strudel. Preheat your oven to 400 degrees Fahrenheit (200 degrees Celsius) and gather these ingredients:

> 7 ounces defrosted pastry, rolled out very thin
> 5 ounces chicory, washed and shredded
> 1 onion, finely chopped
> 1 cup Caerphilly cheese, grated
> 1 egg, beaten

Fold pastry into an oblong, twice. Roll firmly until thin again. Combine chicory, cheese, and onion. Spoon mixture into center of pastry. Brush edges of pastry with half the egg. Roll up pastry and crimp shut. Cut 1-inch slices into top of pastry. Bake for 40 minutes until golden. Serve hot or cold.

Your Wanderings . . .

Chicory is a wildflower that blooms each season longer than most; its blue flowers can be found June through October in fields and along roadsides. Part of the aster family, its flowers can be light blue, white, or pink.

9

Columbine

Aquilegia Cœrulea

*F*ew people can see this wildflower without commenting on its unique blossom. The columbine flower is shaped like the head and neck of a dove, and the spurs of the flower look like a quintet of doves bent down to drink at a fountain. The English name also stems from the word *columba*, which means "dove."

Yet Native Americans knew and used the columbine much earlier than the English and have many legends about the flower, including one tribe's warning to children: "If you pick it, rain will come." Tribes never used the columbine as food, but they did use it as a medicine. They chewed the plant's leaves and spit them onto burns, and they boiled its roots and used the liquid to cure diarrhea.

Though this wildflower's unusual bloom still draws comment, today its name makes us pause. Few of us can hear "columbine" without remembering the tragedy in a Colorado high school—and longing for peace.

My Wonderings . . .

> As soon as Jesus was baptized, he went up out of the water. At that moment heaven was opened, and he saw the Spirit of God descending like a dove and lighting on him. And a voice from heaven said, "This is my Son, whom I love; with him I am well pleased."
>
> Matthew 3:16–17

I use symbols. I place a ring on my left hand's third finger and a circled *c* on my writings. I even wear an apple pin when I teach.

God uses symbols too. He had his people put a bronze serpent on a staff and a pile of rocks in a river. He told a prophet to bury a sash and commanded his disciples to break bread and drink wine. He even used a dove as a symbol for his Spirit.

Is it possible God places symbols in his creation too? Do the dove-shaped petals of his columbine serve more purpose than helping bees make honey and causing folks to say, "Oh, that's beautiful"?

I think so.

I don't believe it's happenstance that a wildflower's petal shape looks like the bird God used to embody his Spirit. Surely he knew that even in a mountain paradise, we would need a gentle reminder of the comfort and hope found in his Spirit.

Your Wanderings . . .

Anytime June through August you'll find the adaptable columbine blooming in meadows and woodlands, along alpine rock beds, on dry, talus slopes, and in moist, shady forests, especially aspen groves.

Seed Money

Long the subject of poets, the red, blue, yellow, and orange flowering columbine can grace any garden or bouquet. In fact, the poet John Parkinson wrote in the 1600s, "No garden would willingly be without them."

Start your own columbine flowers—cheaply, the old-fashioned way—indoors. Use a cardboard egg carton. Tear off the lid, fill the egg holes with good potting soil, plant columbine seeds (nurseries carry wild or domestic varieties) in each egg hole, and place the carton in a sunny spot or window. Water carefully each day. When the seedlings are one inch high, gently tear or cut each egg compartment from the carton and plant them still in the egg holder where there's a good mix of shade and sun. The cardboard will disintegrate quickly, and flowers will return each year without reseeding.

The plants thrive in a mixture of shade and sun. Once they are established, you'll find the columbine's beauty as soothing as did the poet Ralph Waldo Emerson, who wrote, "A woodland walk, a quest for river grapes, a mocking thrush, a wild rose or rock-living columbine salve my worst wounds."

10
Common Camass

Camassia Quamash

*S*tar-shaped blossoms of deep blue line the tall stalk of common camass. A few stamens,[7] wearing what appears to be an oversized yellow shoe, protrude from each center. When blooming, these flowers can transform a moist meadow into an ocean of blue. In fact, this is just how explorer Meriwether Lewis first spotted a camass field, recording in his journal on June 12, 1806, "At a short distance it resembles lakes of fine clear water."

Their prolific numbers and edible bulbs made camass a mainstay in the diet of many Native American tribes. Women dug out the two-inch rounds with a stick before the plants bloomed. Then they pit-roasted the bulbs or hand-pressed the bulbs into cakes to be dried for later use. The bulbs' high food value caused tribes to travel long distances to obtain them, and tribes even fought for possession of areas where camass grew in the thousands.

My Wonderings . . .

> The people went around gathering it [manna], and then ground it in a handmill or crushed it in a mortar. They cooked it in a pot or made it into cakes. And it tasted like something made with olive oil.
>
> Numbers 11:8

Unless we're farmers or gardeners, we don't watch dirt-covered seeds sprout into tall cornstalks or large yellow pumpkins. We don't fill feed troughs and see wobbly legged calves become massive thousand-pound steers. Instead we pick our clean vegetables from expertly stacked bins and select our plastic-wrapped, cut meat from packed coolers. As a result, it is easy to forget that God provides our food.

Our market shelves would be bare without water, soil, and sunshine to make crops and animal feed. And although agriculturists and scientists have helped food production, they still need the raw elements that God provides to produce it.

Native American tribes realized their camass depended on good rains, and they directed prayers toward the heavens. And the Old Testament Hebrews recognized God as the source of their manna. But what about me?

When I chew a mouthful of buttered potato or savor a chicken drumstick, do I give credit to almighty God? Do I truly thank him for the incredible variety and abundance of food I have?

Your Wanderings . . .

Look for this low-growing perennial in moist soils during the late winter and early spring. Growth begins when the tiny

Bulbs of Paradise

Native Americans would move to quamash (camass) fields in the early autumn for this staple. Some people would harvest the bulbs, which are about the same size as a small onion. (Indeed, camass belongs to the onion family, but it doesn't taste like it.) Others would dig a pit, line it with boulders, fill it with wood, and set fire to it. The fire would heat the boulders on which the harvested bulbs would be placed; all would be covered with earth and the bulbs left to cook slowly for two days. Rich in starch, the bulbs develop a sweet flavor when slowly baked. They can also be eaten raw but have a gummy texture. Once the pit was opened, the feasting began—and what a feast!

For those who don't own or have access to their own plot of land, try this: Wrap several cups of camass bulbs in tinfoil and bury them in the bottom of a campfire or fireplace just before bedtime. Cover the foil bundle with a couple inches of dirt at the campfire or coals in the fireplace and stoke the fire so it's hot on top. As your fire dies overnight, the camass bulbs roast and will be done by morning.

grasslike stems poke from between wet cracks and crevices on rocky outcrops.

Usually in April, the clusters of blue-purple flowers emerge, often mingling with the yellow of spring gold and western buttercup. Camass likes full sun and survives in poor soils on rocky outcrops, making it ideal for use in northern rock gardens, sunny garden edges, and sunny wet spots near ponds.

11

Dandelion

Taraxacum Officinale

*M*any of us would like to see less of dandelions! We even think of the dandelion not as a flower but instead as a pesky weed. However, children love the dandelion's bright and simple beauty, and make a game of blowing on its puffy seed head to watch in fascination as it bursts and feathery pods float in all directions.

Contrary to us with our gardening woes, children have more truly captured the truth about dandelions. Few plants provide like this one. If you're hungry, it has more food value than most green vegetables—being nutritionally rich and high in magnesium, calcium, potassium, and vitamins A and C—and can be cooked or enjoyed as fresh greens in a salad. If you're thirsty, dandelion blossoms can be made into a wine or its roots roasted for a hot drink. Early settlers looked to the hearty dandelion for nutrition when vegetables were scarce; and even earlier, Native Americans used dandelions medicinally as a laxative and diuretic.

My Wonderings . . .

> But God chose the foolish things of this world . . . and the despised things—and the things that are not—to nullify the things that are, so that no one may boast before him.

> 1 Corinthians 1:27–29

I barely noticed her at first. I was the new wife of a widowed pastor, and I just thought she made a few extra dollars each month by vacuuming our small country church and cleaning its bathrooms. But as the days passed, I began to see Kathy, really see her. She bought and picked up supplies. She drove the church van to youth events. She volunteered to clean up after our women's meetings. She even took older folks to their doctor appointments. Nothing she does ranks as grand or boast worthy—it's just needed.

It's easy to avoid lowly transporting and toilet cleaning jobs. They hardly seem like "great things for God." But I've begun to wonder. Though Kathy struggles to share even in a small group, people know and speak well of her. Though newcomers like myself initially see her as the "custodian," it doesn't take long to realize her value to our church. No wonder Jesus said that in serving, a person becomes great.

Your Wanderings . . .

You won't need to go far to find a dandelion or two as they bloom in lawns, fields, and along roadsides almost year round in temperate climates. Flowers bloom March through December. Roots can be harvested year-round, even in winter; young leaves are best picked before the flower forms.

Dandelions can grace your table in a child's bouquet—or as part of the meal.

For a salad of dandelion greens: Pick young leaves where no herbicides have been used. The tender crown found below the ground can be eaten too. To clean and lift any hidden bugs, place the greens in a gallon container, cover them with cold water and two tablespoons of salt to set for half an hour. Lift greens out of the water and rinse before placing on a cutting board to dry.

To enjoy as a cooked vegetable: Gather the roots. Peel, slice, and boil them in two water baths to remove the bitterness. After draining, steam them like spinach, or cook in a saucepan with a tight lid and two inches of cold water over medium heat for 10 to 15 minutes until the greens are well wilted. Do not drain until just before serving. Add a bit of vinegar, butter, and salt to taste.

For a delicate-tasting, golden, clear jelly: Make this in the spring for a taste of summer on the first snowy morning.

1 quart fresh, bright dandelion flowers
2 tablespoons lemon juice
5½ cups sugar
1 package (1¾ ounce) powdered pectin
paraffin to seal

Using an enamel or stainless steel pan, boil the dandelions in 2 quarts of water for 3 to 5 minutes; cool and strain, pressing the liquid out of the flowers gently. Measure 3 cups of the liquid; add lemon juice and pectin. Put into a deep jelly kettle and bring to a boil. Add sugar and stir to mix well. Stir and boil for 2½ minutes or until the mixture sheets from a wooden spoon. Pour into jelly glasses and seal with melted paraffin when cool.

12

Elephant Head
Pedicularis Groenlandica

*E*lephant head's spire of purple-pink flowers appears each summer in high, wet meadows and along streams. Feathery, fernlike leaves decorate the lower half of its stalk and surround its base.

Many hikers who spot this wildflower will stop in their tracks to look at the crowded rows of blossoms along the top half of the stalk. Voila! Immediately they know how the plant got its name. The individual flowers look exactly like a small, colored elephant head with its trunk raised. Yet this unusual shape does more than mimic a zoo and circus animal. It aids in pollination while reducing the chance of crossbreeding with other plants.

My Wonderings . . .

> The heavens are yours, and yours also the earth;
> you founded the world and all that is in it.

> Psalm 89:11

The contrast between a huge, gray-hided, trunk-swinging elephant and the delicate raceme[8] of light purple blooms on this plant assaults anyone who compares the two. Yet they look alike. How is that possible? How could a fragile North American mountain flower resemble a gigantic mammal from Asia and Africa?

Could it be—they both had the same designer?

It makes me smile to think of God fashioning these two look-alikes. I can imagine his delight at taking such opposites and giving them the same rounded head, floppy big ears, and upturned trunk. If I'd watched the duo's creation, I'd have thought, *Wow, you sure can't miss God's handprint in this inconceivable combination!*

Yet some people do.

The truth is not changed. The One who designed and made the elephant also designed and made its floral counterpart. Together, they whisper, "See what God did? Isn't he awe inspiring?"

Your Wanderings . . .

You might have to get your feet wet in mid-June to late July if you want to find elephant head blooms along streams, bogs, and damp meadows at middle to high elevations. Elephant head blooms are especially prevalent along streams in Yel-

Bring home an elephant flower from the wild—on film. You'll add spice to your photos if you go close-up. (When shooting with a macro lens, the depth of field is very minimal, so use the lens "stopped down" to f11 or f16, if the lighting conditions permit.) You'll also capture all the flower's intricate detail, color, and textures.

Flowers are at their best in the early morning. The slanting rays of the sun highlight the texture of every petal and grain of pollen. Use a 31b warming filter to punch up red shades, warm up a shadowy forest floor, or take off the bluish chill of an overcast day.

Experimenting with depth of field adds pizzazz too: an f-stop of 5.6 or 4 can help blur a background to eliminate distracting clutter or isolate one blossom from the group, while an f-stop of 11 or 16 gives you a deeper range in focus.

lowstone National Park; on any visit, a hike is worth it to examine this unique blossom. Afterward, you can honestly say, "I saw a pink elephant."

13

English Daisy

Bellis Perennis

Unlike its larger relatives, the English daisy nestles close to the ground. Its button-size flowers sit on or just above a clump of flat, oval leaves. Like all its wild daisy cousins, this small "he-loves-me-he-loves-me-not" blossom flourishes in open spaces. Its familiar white rays and bright yellow center can bloom year-round if sunshine peeks through winter skies for a few days. No wonder folks named this type of flower "day's-eye" or daisy.

One of its favorite growing places is domestic lawns, and without encouragement a single plant can soon become a dozen.

Though English daisy potions have been used as an aches-and-pains cure-all and as a potherb, the flower is best known as poetry fodder. Wordsworth, Tennyson, and Burns used this petite, pretty bloom in their writings.

My Wonderings . . .

Then God said, "Let the earth sprout vegetation: plants yielding seed, *and* fruit trees on the earth bearing fruit after their kind with seed in them"; and it was so.

Genesis 1:11 NASB

English daisies flourish in my large country front lawn. When the sun shines, I've seen them poke their cheerful little blooms above the best fertilized and most luxuriant green grass. Their polka-dotting of my landscaping efforts does tempt me to give them a good dose of weed killer. Though perky additions to my lawn, these little wildflowers won't arrange themselves to my satisfaction. Why can't they edge the lawn around the big oak tree or line the walkway up to the front porch? No, they just pop up wherever.

But so far I've left them alone. They remind me that my idea of order is not always God's idea of order. I want problems to end first and then to learn the lessons. God often teaches the lesson and then ends the problem. I prefer loving people who are loving. God says I need to love the unlovely.

Since his order is not always my preference, I need my English daisies. Though scattered in non-scaped randomness, each one is obeying God's order—reproducing after its own kind.

Your Wanderings . . .

According to an old proverb, "When you can put your foot on seven daisies, summer is come." Indeed, the daisy begins blooming in spring and spreads increasingly through summer

We Love Them, We Love Them Not . . .

Whether you find your daisies in the garden, on the lawn, or in a cheap bundle from the grocery store (they're almost always in stock through summer), gather a bunch for this fun sunny-day project with children.

Make a daisy chain. With a fingernail or dull knife, you can easily split daisy stems, allowing you to slip the stem of another bloom through it. Keep going, and soon everyone will be wearing daisy necklaces and crowns. Take pictures of your fanciful fun to remember long after the daisies have wilted.

into early autumn. It can be found in lawns, in fields, and along roadsides and is celebrated the world over. In fact, the English poet Chaucer once noted how the daisy's common name is a corruption of the wildflower's old English name, "day's-eye." Speaking of the bloom's popularity, especially for making into daisy chains, he wrote, "By reason men it call maie, the Daisie is else the Eye of the Daie."

Fireweed

14

Fireweed

Epilobium Angustifolium

*N*o soil is too poor or too thin for fireweed's tower of purple-pink flowers. Found all over the world, it has many uses. Russian peasants brewed a popular drink from it called "kaporie." People in Europe steamed its young shoots like asparagus, while Eskimos ate its roots uncooked. Native Americans wove its downy seed bursts with wool and duck feathers into blankets.

Like those who put this plant to use, fireweed is a pioneer, often appearing first in burned or cleared areas. After World War II, bombings left England scorched and broken, and bright spikes of fireweed, also called blooming sally, were the first reminders to the people that their land would be restored.

My Wonderings . . .

The LORD has anointed Me . . .
To console those who mourn in Zion,
To give them beauty for ashes,
The oil of joy for mourning,
The garment of praise for the spirit of heaviness.

Isaiah 61:1, 3 NKJV

Fireweed's double names are not without reason. Today, those who maintain neatly kept yards and fields see this hardy plant as little more than a colorful weed. But for those who depended upon its uses or saw its blooms among charred stumps or bombed buildings, it was a beautiful blooming sally, a flower that delighted their eyes and eased their hearts.

In the same way, the ashes of pain and the rubble of evil in our lives can change our perspective on day-to-day things. The loving people we took for granted become our support. The encouraging notes we used to toss become treasures tucked within our Bible's pages. The kind words we barely heard become soul salve. And the God we knew only as much as our time allowed incredibly becomes our peace, our comfort, our heavenly Father.

Your Wanderings . . .

From June through August, look for fireweed's blooms in high, mountainous, sunny spots, especially on burned-over land, in clear cuts, in cities, or on vacant lots. The violet or rose-purple flowers open gradually. A great spike of fifteen to fifty or more flowers adorns the stem, each flower on its own stalk, from midsummer to fall. Bees near fireweed colo-

As a willow herb, fireweed can be a unique addition to your tea selections. High in both vitamin A and C, the spring shoots brew into a mild, light yellow-green beverage reminiscent of a traditional green tea but with a hint of sweetness. Medicinally known for its mild laxative effect, fireweed is purported to relieve stomachache. Because it is slightly sweet, it benefits very little from the addition of sugar or milk and is enjoyable, hot or cold, all on its own or mixed with other tea herbs like mint, nettle, or chamomile.

Make a blend as Native Americans and even Eastern Russians have done for centuries—and as documented by the Royal British Columbia Museum in Vancouver. Snap the plant off at its base and then strip the leaves. You'll need one cup of fresh or dry leaves for a winter brew. If fresh, look for young leaves, rinse them well, and lay them flat on a dry surface.

Steep the leaves in boiling water for about five minutes and then strain them off.

nies make a rich-tasting, dark-colored honey from the plant's pollen and nectar. In winter, the spent stalks die and become like dry straw.

15
Forget-Me-Not
Hackelia Floribunda

*T*he branched clusters of forget-me-not's tiny blue flowers love moist areas. They frequently decorate stream banks, meadows, and thickets. A European native, this small wildflower was brought to the American West by settlers. Its different varieties grow from northern New Mexico to Alaska.

Though it looks delicate, long, cold winters don't bother it. Many types of forget-me-nots are also called "stickweed" because of the seeds they produce. Each seed has small barbs that stick to clothes and fur. As a result, pioneers, Indians, and even modern-day hikers find it hard to "forget" this flower and leave it behind.

My Wonderings . . .

Can a mother forget the baby at her breast
  and have no compassion on the child she has borne?
Though she may forget,
  I will not forget you!
See, I have engraved you on the palms of my hands.

Isaiah 49:15–16

Forgetting comes naturally to me. I forget where I put my car keys. I forget the monthly Sunday school meeting. I even forget the name of a longtime friend I haven't seen for a while.

I know God is not like me. In normal, everyday moments, it doesn't even cross my mind that he might let something slip by or his mind "blank out."

But in dark moments, when my heart cries, and only circumstances seem to answer, I can ask God, "Where are you? What are you doing? Have you forgotten me?"

My feelings are real. My questions are honest.

But can my God change? Can he forget me? Can he not see my nail scars in his hands?

Your Wanderings . . .

Look for forget-me-not blooms late June through July in foothills and moist meadows near coniferous forests. Alaska claims the alpine forget-me-not, which is sky blue in color and about the size of a quarter, as its official state flower.

Pools of Petals

Forget-me-nots make a wonderful addition to garden fountains, because they love partly sunny/partly shady, moist areas, require little attention, survive until first frost, and will soon produce a tousle of blue beauties in "pools" around your trickling water.

You'll find a larger, domestic variety of forget-me-nots sold at most nurseries. Wild ones are more challenging to transplant, but it can be done. For earlier blooms, start seeds indoors a few weeks before the last frost in your area. Cover seeds lightly with one-eighth inch of garden soil, space them four to five inches apart, and thin seedlings to ten inches apart.

Children especially love the flower's soft "mouse ear" leaves, so called because of their covering in a fine, fibrous "hair."

Foxglove

16

Foxglove

Digitalis Purpurea

oxglove's long blossoms look like a glove's cut-off fingertips. Dozens hang from the plant's tall stem, forming a raceme of colorful beauty. Ranging from white to deep purple, each tubular blossom has an inner "lip" dotted with a contrasting color.

Though originally a domestic flower, foxglove "escaped" and began flourishing in the wild. Native Americans recognized the striking plant as an intruder and did not find uses for it, but doctors did.

Whether wild or domestic, foxglove provides a lifesaving drug. The heart stimulant digitalis comes from its leaves. Small quantities of the harvested drug stimulate heartbeat and improve circulation. By 1787, doctors in the United States were prescribing digitalis. But even earlier, the noted statesman Benjamin Franklin used it while a diplomat in England.

My Wonderings . . .

Jesus replied: "'Love the Lord your God with all your heart and with all your soul and with all your mind.' This is the first and greatest commandment."

Matthew 22:37–38

My heart stimulant did not come from a plant or out of a bottle. She came with a gray bun, thick-lensed glasses, and sturdy shoes.

She asked our young women's Bible study, "Were you ever separated from your husband while engaged to him? Do you remember how you looked for the mailman, waiting eagerly for his letters? How you read and reread them?"

I remembered. I longed for every letter. I soaked up every word.

She interrupted my memories by holding out her worn, open Bible and saying with a sincerity that even her thick glasses could not hide, "That's how you should feel about this book. It's God's love letter to you."

Her words took hold of my mind, my heart. That's how I wanted to love God. I wanted to see his Word as a love letter. My spiritual heart thumped with desire, and I cried out to God, "I want to be more than a good Christian. I want to fall in love with you."

That day my love affair with God began.

Your Wanderings . . .

From the garden walls of William Randolph Hearst's grand castle San Simeon in California to the crevices of rocky hill-

Best Bee-autiful

Foxglove, the wildflower, is a common garden escape (found at any nursery) that creates an aura of strength and dignity. Plant a row of foxglove in partially shaded areas, as a tall, colorful addition along picket fences or light-colored homes, among shrubs in solid beds, or as a border along stream or wood edges.

Since they usually won't survive to bloom a second year, foxgloves can be removed after they release their seeds for next year's plants (or right after flowering if you don't want them to reseed). Another trick is to cut the flowering stalk after blooming so more shoots will grow and bloom later in the season.

Caution: If you have small children who might be tempted to eat plants, avoid foxglove. The unprocessed digitalis in it is poisonous. As many a park service guide has warned: "You should only ingest foxglove if you are a bee."

sides, dry hilly pastures, and logged-off clearings, you'll find foxglove in bloom June through July. The stems can stand quite tall—three to six feet—making this toxic plant hard to miss.

17

Indian Pipe

Monotropa Uniflora

*E*arly settlers gave Indian pipe its name because of how it looks when it first blooms. The bell-shaped blossom stands straight out from its stem. Only as it ages does the flower droop, giving it a nodding-bell look.

In contrast, Native Americans named this plant because of its unusual qualities. They called it "ghost flower." It nestles into the darkest parts of wooded areas yet has an ethereal beauty. White and waxy with a bluish translucence, the elegant plant hardly seems fitting for the decaying forest floor. But without it, the flower could not exist.

Unlike most other wildflowers, Indian pipe does not need sunshine to grow. It is a saprophyte and has the ability to transform the forest's rotting vegetation into spotless white. But the white won't last if you touch it. Contact with human skin causes the plant's delicate tissue to turn black.

My Wonderings . . .

Come, let's talk this over! says the Lord; no matter how deep the stain of your sins, I can take it out and make you as clean as freshly fallen snow. Even if you are stained as red as crimson, I can make you white as wool!

Isaiah 1:18 TLB

The first time I read about saprophytes, I shook my head in disbelief. It didn't seem possible. How could something so beautiful come from something so awful? Besides the contents of a garbage can, nothing disgusts me like rotting vegetation. Whether I see, smell, or accidentally touch it, I jerk back in revulsion. Yet from such a vile heap comes one of the forest's most exquisite and delicate flowers.

If ever God provided a living illustration of what his transforming power can do, it's in Indian pipe's elegant, white, bell-shaped flower. No person, no matter how debased by evil, is beyond God's transforming touch.

Your Wanderings . . .

Coming across a cluster of Indian pipes, deep in the woods or shady places, can be an eerie, almost shocking experience June through September. The bloom's pale bluish white flesh in the dark of the midsummer woods looks ghostly. This albino is somewhat closely related to the dogwoods, heaths, and even the evergreen laurels and rhododendrons; like some of these cousins, Indian pipe has learned ways to take advantage of other life forms in order to live in places where few plants

Indian pipe cannot be transplanted and ends up more in legends and stories than stew pots or medicine bags. Still, this hard-to-find plant deserves a quest. When camping or hiking in August, make an effort to find and kneel in study at a clump of these unique blooms in deeply shaded parts of the woods. Reflect on an ode to the Indian pipe by Mary Potter Thacher Higginson (1844–1941).

In shining groups, each stem a pearly ray,
Weird flecks of light within the shadowed wood,
They dwell aloof, a spotless sisterhood.
No Angelus, except the wild bird's lay,
Awakes these forest nuns; yet night and day,
Their heads are bent, as if in prayerful mood.
A touch will mar their snow, and tempests rude
Defile; but in the mist fresh blossoms stray
From spirit-gardens, just beyond our ken.
Each year we seek their virgin haunts, to look
Upon new loveliness, and watch again
Their shy devotions near the singing brook;
Then, mingling in the dizzy stir of men,
Forget the vows made in that clustered nook.

A Garden for Genuflecting

could survive. Indeed, Indian pipe sometimes is associated with death because the plant often grows near decaying vegetation, and once plucked, blooms will melt in your hand, quickly turning black.

18
Inside-out Flower
Vancouveria Hexandra

*U*pside-down fits this tiny white flower better than
inside-out. It looks like someone picked off all the
plant's blooms and glued them back on to their threadlike
stems upside down! The flower's flared tube comes off the
stem while the narrow base dangles in midair. Viewers have
compared the reverse blooms to ballerinas on tiptocs, wearing frilly tutus.

The fact that inside-out flower belongs to the same botanical family as the shrub Oregon grape (see chapter 22 on page
97) also adds to its oddity. It hardly seems possible that this
fine-stemmed, tiny-flowered plant could be related to one
that reaches six feet in height and has a woody trunk, spiked
holly-type leaves, and brilliant yellow flowers. Yet both are
members of the barberry family.

My Wonderings . . .

You created my inmost being;
  you knit me together in my mother's womb.
I praise you because I am fearfully and wonderfully
          made;
  your works are wonderful.

Psalm 139:13–14

My husband would love to go to Scotland. "Just once in my life," he says, "I'd like to go someplace where I don't stand out."

Born with orange-red hair, easy-to-freckle fair skin, and a stocky, no-neck build, he has never fit in. Of course, his school years were the worst, and names like "Carrot Top" and "Red" still don't sit well. But I love his full head of now strawberry blond hair and his broad chest. And I like the fact that I can always find him in a store. I know God made my husband just right. Even the rough childhood he endured has produced a tender, compassionate heart that makes him a wonderful pastor.

It's easy to concentrate on what makes us different or odd. But when I see my husband's handsome red hair, I think, *Oh, Lord, you are such a wonderful creator.*

No matter how it may appear, God doesn't do things upside down or inside out. He does things perfectly.

Your Wanderings . . .

Found May through June in moist, shady forests, often at edges and openings, the inside-out flower's blooms may jump out at you as tiny white ballerinas dancing along the wooded floor. Light green leaves shaped like duck feet seem appropriate for its soggy clime; panicles of white flowers, with stamens and pistils[9] pointing down from petals flared back like shooting stars, give the plant its name.

Second Nature

Though inside-out flower has few recorded uses, it does make a wonderful ground cover in shaded areas of your yard if you live west of the Cascade or Sierra Mountains. It spreads from a wide-running rhizome,[10] so be sure to scoop up soil with the wildflower when you transplant it. A hardy perennial in the barberry family, inside-out flower especially likes the company of redwoods, ferns, salal, and rhododendrons.

As a remembrance of inside-out flowers seen—and left—in the wild, select a leaf or fern near it for a botanical print to make for your home. On off-white or sepia-toned paper, print the horticultural name of the plant on the lower center of the page. Load the paper in a color photocopier, position the leaf on the copying table, photocopy, and there you have it—botanical art on a dime (though looking much more fine and rich), ready to matte and frame or use for a greeting card.

Lupine

19

Lupine

Lupinus Polyphyllus

This lush variety of lupine sends up tall spires of deep blue blossoms, but a half dozen other varieties of this wildflower decorate the United States. Their blooms come in blue, pink, and yellow hues. Their leaves vary from smooth, shiny green to rough, hairy silver, and their size ranges from just off the ground to five feet.

Yet lupines can't be missed. All varieties have spires of pea-shaped flowers with round leaflets beneath.

Few other flowers grow in the poor soil where lupines flourish. Rocky hillsides, graveled road edges, and even desert sands provide enough nutrients. And they don't just grow—they enrich the soil by releasing nitrogen into it.

Lupine has staying power too. In 1967 botanists discovered frozen seeds, estimated to be more than ten thousand years old. When planted, the seeds germinated within forty-eight hours.

My Wonderings . . .

> Blessed *be* the God and Father of our Lord Jesus Christ, the Father of mercies and God of all comfort, who comforts us in all our tribulation, that we may be able to comfort those who are in any trouble.
>
> 2 Corinthians 1:3–4 NKJV

I must have a little lupine in me. I wish I grew and nourished others in rich, gentle circumstances. But in truth, I often grow and touch those around me for the best after life takes on a barren harshness.

When I require wisdom for difficulties, solace for pain, and courage to go on, my need for God presses beyond the surface of my life. Prayer becomes earnest one-on-One, not just a quick SOS and table grace. Bible reading becomes a heart quest, not just a quiet time. I must find God in my desert.

And after I do, others want to hear the story. Listening to my heartaches and mistakes, they identify. And pondering the divine moment when my problem didn't disappear but God became clear, they leave nourished, somehow fed by seeing him do a miracle in my desert.

Your Wanderings . . .

The blue to violet-pink lupine blooms in woods, fields, and along hillsides and roadsides in early summer (May through early July). Look for long spikes of flowers that are pea-shaped or butterfly-like on stems three feet tall and higher. Notice over time how, from the pealike blooms, long pods develop and eventually dry, still dangling from the spires. Sometimes

Nuke a Lupe

Instead of waiting weeks to air dry and press wildflowers from the fields, do this instantly in your microwave using a press such as Microfleur. (Microwave flower press prices range from thirty-five dollars to fifty dollars; see www.gardeners.com.)

Thin, fairly flat petals like those from a wild pansy or violet work best, but all—even the fluttery lupine—can be preserved well this way, holding both color and texture.

Place the blooms, stems, and leaves on fabric liners that draw moisture from the flowers to expel through vents in the plates of the press. Then experiment with drying time (a couple minutes or less) and power level based on the density of the flowers being pressed. Start with just a few seconds at a low power and increase as necessary. The result is an everlasting keepsake to use on greeting cards, bookmarks, journals, or as a romantic surprise on a particular page of a favorite book.

the pods simply open, leaving propagation to the birds and wind. At other times, they burst, flinging seeds yards away from the mother plant.

20

Morning Glory

Ipomoea Purpurea

A whole orchestra of pink-white trumpets stand out on morning glory's hardy vine. Without sound, they play for the summer sun, unfurling their flared tubes only when night's darkness gives way to morning's light. Though this wildflower requires sunshine to bloom, its vine knows no such limitations.

At the height of its season, you'll find it wrapped around tree trunks, lampposts, and fence railings. The green tendrils grab a tight hold onto anything near them, sometimes choking other plants or pulling posts over. As a result, many people call this wildflower "bindweed."

The flower's second name also reflects its copious root system, which makes it difficult to get rid of once it is established. But this tenacity has a beneficial side. The plant's tough root network holds on to the soil and prevents erosion. It has even been planted to keep sand from washing out to sea.

My Wonderings . . .

I give them eternal life, and they shall never perish; no one can snatch them out of my hand. My Father, who has given them to me, is greater than all; no one can snatch them out of my Father's hand.

John 10:28–29

The idea that I am kept in God's hands has always comforted me. When teased as a child, when misunderstood as a wife, when overwhelmed as a mother, I could picture gigantic hands wrapped around me.

But sometimes I didn't feel totally safe. Didn't Solomon slip out of God's hands at the end of his life? Unconsciously, I changed the verse to read, "No person, except me, is able to snatch . . ."

Then one day I tried to take myself from his hands. Torn apart by an evil touching my life, I cried, "God, if I knew how to give you up, I would." Inwardly, I ran as fast and as far as I could. But like Solomon, in the end, I could only say, "Fear God . . . for this is man's all" (Eccles. 12:13 NKJV).

Can I really ever overcome the power of God's almighty grasp?

Your Wanderings . . .

July through August you'll find the pink, purple, blue, or white blooms of wild morning glories along roadsides, covering hillsides, and as staples in many a flower garden. Just follow the hummingbirds, who particularly love the "heavenly blue" variety. Flower sizes vary as well, from giant trumpet-like blooms to more compact models. Flowers may last only

Secret Garden Glories

If you don't already have some memory of climbing a morning glory trellis or seeing the flower's first unfurling spirals greet the sun, you can make one.

Morning glories root easily and need little care. Seeds can be purchased at a variety of stores, and roots are especially fond of rain shed, so if your yard has a slope or incline this is the perfect flower to plant at the base. For the earliest possible blooms, start seeds in a sunny window four to six weeks before transplanting outdoors. Then plant a half inch to one inch deep and six to ten inches apart. Plants will germinate in a week to ten days. Soak seeds overnight in warm water before planting for faster growth.

Create a private nook in your garden by arranging several poles or strings in a tepee formation. Plant morning glory seeds at the base of each pole and watch sprouts begin to climb. By midsummer, you'll have a perfect reading spot, surrounded by these delicate blooms and leafy vines.

one day, but the plants are prolific bloomers, especially when spent blooms are pinched off—new ones will come back bigger and brighter.

21

Nootka Rose

Rosa Nutkana

*N*othing about this wildflower puts on a big show. Five pink, round, overlapping petals form small blooms measuring only one to three inches. A sparse cluster of thin stamens fill in each bloom's center. Yet this many-flowered shrub does as much to decorate its wild habitat as the fullest, deepest-colored, prize-winningest domestic rose does for any garden.

Beauty only lends to the allure of wild roses. Their blooms and greenery produce a sensuous fragrance that makes country walkers and outdoor hikers look around for its source. In addition, a berrylike seedpod or "hip" forms after the blooms disappear and the plant goes to seed. These hips make a unique and good-tasting jam or jelly that is rich with vitamin C.

My Wonderings . . .

I am full, having received from Epaphroditus the things which were *sent* from you, a sweet-smelling aroma, an acceptable sacrifice, well pleasing to God.

Philippians 4:18–19 NKJV

I like seeing the glass half full, making lemonade from lemons, and in general living out the other make-you-feel-good clichés. But I know from experience that a positive attitude doesn't remove life's pain or answer its whys.

However, I found something that helped when I grieved my first husband's death. We'd married young and had our kids early, always saying, "When we're forty-five, the kids will be grown and we'll have the time and money to do what we want." That dream died with my husband before we reached thirty-five years old.

When I thought about our lost dream, I'd grieve so hard. But one day I read about sweet-smelling, well-pleasing sacrifices to God. In my mind, I pictured an altar to God, alive with burning flames. With care, I picked up our dream for the future and laid it on the fire. It burned up, disappearing in a waft of smoke that lifted to heaven. God watched me bring this precious dream to him, and knowing how much it cost me, he delighted in its sweet smell and found it well pleasing.

My verse-based mental picture went far beyond my preference for feel-good clichés. It transformed my loss into divine pleasure.

Follow your nose to find the sweet, cinnamon-like scent from dense thickets of Nootka rose growing at forest edges, in meadows, and along country highways and beachfronts.

Blooms come early in June (sometimes May), and hummingbirds and bees feed on the nectar and pollen. Birds love the thorny branches for cover and the green hips for food (especially towhees, thrashers, and Steller's jays, who will continue to dine through autumn, after the rose loses its leaves, and winter, when hips turn an orange scarlet).

Flower-Powered

Dried wild rose petals, hips, and leaves make wonderful potpourri additions and food garnishes. They can be gathered in the fall, and folklore has it that the hips are a food supplement, tastier and richer in vitamin C after the first frost. They are indeed an incredible source of vitamin C, far richer than oranges. So during the first and second World Wars, people were advised to gather and prepare them as a vitamin supplement.

For potpourri: Place rose petals, hips, and leaves on a rack in a low-temperature oven (200 degrees Fahrenheit or so). It won't take long for the petals and then the leaves to dry. The hips will take the longest. You can also use commercial plant-drying crystals.

For an edible garnish: Rose petals (free of pesticides) make a striking addition to cream soup or on a dessert plate. The bitter white base should be trimmed off before using.

22
Oregon Grape
Berberis Repens

*S*hiny hollylike leaves (without the prickles) backdrop Oregon grape's brilliant cluster of yellow flowers. The rounded blooms never open flat, allowing them to bunch together like grapes on the two or three stems that protrude above the leaves. One variety towers up to six feet tall, while another one stays bush size and sends out creepers,[11] underground rhizomes, that can start new plants.

Native Americans and pioneers used the plant's bark and roots for treatments to ease sores, coughs, and stomach disorders; they ate and dried the dark berries that formed after the flowers bloomed. Today jams and jellies are still made from the lush fruit.

But Oregon grape is best known as a dye plant. Its berries turn wool an attractive blue, while its roots yield an excellent yellow dye that can even color basket fibers.

My Wonderings . . .

Make the ephod of gold, and of blue, purple and scarlet yarn,
and of finely twisted linen—the work of a skilled craftsman.

Exodus 28:6–7

God won't ask me to do something without providing the
means to do it. But as a stepparent, I don't always feel well
provisioned. At one such time, God brought me to this pas-
sage and then set me to thinking.

Yarn, whether made from wool, cotton, or linen, never
comes naturally in gold, blue, purple, or red. Yet this is what
God told the Israelites to use when making the priest's garment. To provide what they needed, the Lord created plants
with the ability to transfer color, such as the Oregon grape.
But that wasn't enough. The Israelites had to find out which
plants could dye yarn and what process to use.

As it happens, the Israelites had been in Egypt for three
hundred years, most of the time working as slaves in agri-
culture and industry. One of the industries included dyeing—
archaeologists have found exquisitely colored fabrics in the
pyramids. By the time the Lord gave his people the command
to make the ephod, he'd provided the means.

Amazed by God's provision, I took a second, more encouraged, look at my stepparenting. Will he not use past circumstances and my knowledge as a mother who has raised four
kids to help me in this new role?

Your Wanderings . . .

You'll find the yellow blooms of the Oregon grape May through
July on mountain slopes and in pine forests. Clumps of yel-

For Juicing and Sprucing

Try home dyeing with these yellow flowers that grow in clusters and yield small, purplish, grapelike berries in the fall.

For a yellowish-green dye great on tea towels and craft projects: Collect four pounds of Oregon grape plant and root in September or October. Remove the bark from the rootstocks with a grater or paring knife. (It's the root that contains the yellow alkaloid berberine.) Boil the shredded bark and roots in five gallons of water for two hours. Strain off plant material and add 1/4 cup raw alum. Boil another 10 minutes, then add 1 pound of pre-wet material (muslin, cotton, yarn). Steep overnight, then rinse and hang to dry.

For tea: Make this decoction to help colds, flu, sinusitis, and infection. In a covered pot, simmer the roots, bark, and seeds for 10 minutes to release their properties, then steep another 15 to 20 minutes. To serve, use 1 tablespoon of decoction to 1 cup water.

1 part dandelion root	1 part burdock root
1 part Oregon grape root	1 part licorice root
1/2 part ginger root	1 part fennel seeds
1/2 part yellow dock root	1 part cinnamon bark

low flowers yield tiny, edible but sour, blue-purple grapes. The shiny, evergreen, ivylike leaves are a common Northwest forest ground cover. Also called "mountain holly" or "Sangre de Cristo" or "creeping mahonia," the plant and its barberry relatives are celebrated worldwide. Italians believe the "holy thorn," as they call it, formed the thorny crown placed on the crucified Jesus's head.

23
Pearly Everlasting
Anaphalis Margaritacea

*I*n fall, when all the other wildflowers begin to turn brown or remain only as naked stems and stalks, you'll find the pearly everlasting still blooming or just beginning to go to seed in pearly clusters.

A naturally dry flower, pearly everlasting has creamy centers, and the surrounding white petals have a paperlike quality. Tiny, soft hairs cover its stem and leaves, giving it a "woolly" touch and protecting it from ants that would climb to get its nectar.

American settlers used the plant as a tobacco substitute, and Native Americans placed it in their steam baths to relieve rheumatism. Today this prolific roadside wildflower is best known for adding a creamy white touch to fall and winter bouquets.

My Wonderings . . .

Before the mountains were brought forth,
Or ever You had formed the earth and the world,
Even from everlasting to everlasting, You *are* God.

Psalm 90:2 NKJV

Time tends to pressure my days. Before my cup of coffee gets cold, time can start harping on my to-do list. And even as I slip in beside my husband at night, it can stick "reminder" Post-it notes on my weary brain. The immediate always demands time because it has so little of it.

But eternity doesn't fall prey to the clock or its pressures. It never runs short or out of time. Minutes and hours don't even exist in eternal dimensions, making calendars, watches, and schedules useless.

Incredibly, I'm stuck between these opposites. I live and breathe in the moment. But the Bible says that if I believe in God's Son, then the One who is everlasting gives me everlasting life. That means that my seventy or eighty years of "clocked living" comprise a mere speck of my life.

This truth doesn't take away my time limits or permanently silence time's voice of pressure. But if I think about living forever . . . and ever . . . and ever, I go down in the morning and reheat my cold coffee. And at night, I dismiss the mental Post-it notes because it feels so good to cuddle against my husband's warm body.

Commonly found in forest openings, pearly everlasting also blooms along roadsides and in fields, from sandy dune lowlands to high in the mountains, June through September. You can't miss the white and woolly stems, with green or grayish hairy leaves. A member of the sunflower family, the pearly everlasting has a flower head that makes a fascinating study as you consider its many tiny flowers, formed much like those of a dandelion or sunflower.

Eternal

Pearly everlasting makes a wonderful addition to any garden, because it grows fast and easily (laughing at fertilizer, rocks, dogs, feet, and bad gardeners), blooms far into the fall—filling in for other plants when they begin to turn brown and droopy—attracts painted lady butterflies, and dries easily as cuts of pearly flower clusters and silvery foliage in bouquets.

To plant: Remove pieces of the rhizome or rooted shoot and replant in a moist and sunny site. Sow the seeds in fall or early spring and transplant seedlings the following fall.

For bouquets: Stiffen the stems with wire and add the blooms to mixed arrangements. To keep blooms from dropping off and intact longer, lightly spritz the white, turbanlike flower heads with hairspray.

To dry: Pick the stalks just before the blooms open, and hang a bouquet upside down by its stems in an arid place. Use the dry stalks to weave into herb wreaths.

24

Pond Lily

Nuphar Polysepala

*T*his aquatic wildflower often adds a yellow ruffle to mountain lakes and marshes. When its large rounded petals unfold, a huge pistil sits in its center. The plant's brightly colored flower "bowls" and big, heart-shaped leaves float on the water's surface. Trapped air and stout stalks hold up the plant, providing resting places for damselflies and dragonflies, frogs and ducklings.

Bears, muskrats, and beavers also like pond lilies, but they root out and eat their rhizomes.

Animals aren't the only ones attracted to this water lily. Native American tribes gathered the many seeds produced by its large pistil. The Klamath Indians even held dances and ceremonies until the "wokas" ripened. Then the women gathered them, grinding most into flour but roasting some like popcorn.

My Wonderings . . .

Whom will he teach knowledge?
And whom will he make to understand the message? . . .
For precept *must be* upon precept, precept upon precept,
Line upon line, line upon line,
Here a little, there a little.

Isaiah 28:9–10 NKJV

I can't think of anything more tedious than gathering seeds—being stooped over for hours, trying to pick enough to make bread for a village. Surely more than one Native American dreaded the job and even wanted to quit.

But then winter snow would cover the last of the berries and roots, and the deer and elk would seek shelter. As the tribal women made woka cakes to feed their families, not a single one regretted filling homemade sacks with the seeds, I'm fairly sure.

Reading my Bible sometimes feels like gathering seeds. After reading and studying it, I can look at what I understand and groan, "Only that much!" It seems like I grasp so little, and it sometimes makes me want to give up.

But when pain makes it impossible for me to think deeply and when other people's words bounce off an emotional wall within me, my mental "sack" of small truths and comforts waits for me to draw upon it. That's when I don't regret one minute spent in the pages of God's book.

Pond Lily

In early spring (usually by May), pond lilies can be found just below the surface of—as their name indicates—ponds and lakes.

By June, the broad, dark green, heart-shaped leaves float on the water's surface or stand above the water, attached by long stems to fleshy rhizomes buried in the mud. By July, the bright yellow, ball-like flowers are in full bloom and emit a strong brandylike fragrance that attracts pollen-seeking insects.

Seed and Feed

Make "popcorn" as Native Americans taught settlers to do with pond lily seeds. If you hike in the fall and spot pond lilies at a lake's edge, gather several quarts of their seeds.

Back home, in a large pan (cast iron works best) melt one half to one cup of butter over high heat and add some of the seeds (store remainder in the refrigerator). Cover the pan with a lid and shake until you hear popping. Keep the pan moving until the popping stops. Remove from the heat immediately and add salt and butter to taste.

25
Queen Anne's Lace
Daucus Carota

The small white blooms of this wildflower join together to form an intricate pattern that looks like living lace. Only a tiny black dot in the middle of its floral umbel[12] belies the illusion. Botanists believe the dot helps bees target the plant for pollination.

In the eighteenth century, ladies of the royal court put Queen Anne's lace's ornate beauty to use by adorning their hair with its intricate blooms and replacing their usual feathers with its fernlike leaves. The wearers paraded the plant before European kings and queens, thus giving it its royal name.

Peasants and early American settlers put Queen Anne's lace to more practical uses. They steeped the plant into a hair rinse that got rid of dandruff and lice. Also, when they pulled up the roots, they smelled something tasty for their stew pots. They simply called the plant "wild carrot."

My Wonderings . . .

But you are a chosen people, a royal priesthood, a holy nation, a people belonging to God, that you may declare the praises of him who called you out of darkness into his wonderful light.

1 Peter 2:9

The Bible tells me I'm royalty—not only part of a royal priesthood but also the daughter of the King of Kings with full access to his heavenly throne room. Yet I often don't feel very royal.

My princess inclinations got left behind in childhood, along with my plastic tiaras and frilly frocks. Somewhere between getting teased as a chubby junior high girl and experiencing the ups and downs of being a wife and mother, I stopped crowning my hair and twirling my dresses.

But my nobility does not depend on me; it depends on what God's Son did on the cross. I am not a princess because I was born with royal blood; I am a princess because royal blood was shed for me.

So when I see lacy round blossoms decorating a meadow or roadside, I never call them "wild carrot." I call them "Queen Anne's lace." They remind me that even if I only feel good enough for the stew pot, I've been given the right to dwell in throne rooms.

Your Wanderings . . .

Queen Anne's lace can be found by scent (roots with the fragrance of carrots) as well as sight June through September. Look in meadows and along roadsides and hillsides for the

Good to the Roots

Considered a medieval vegetable, Queen Anne's lace roots were once commonly served for dinner along with carrots, potatoes, onions, and parsnips.

Try some! Flower clusters can be French fried for a carrot-flavored, attractive dish, and the aromatic seed is used as a flavoring in stews and soups.

When backpacking or camping, look for Queen Anne's lace but be cautious: water hemlock's flower looks like Queen Anne's lace yet is poisonous. Always check for leaves that look like carrot tops and make sure the carrot smell is clearly recognizable in the roots.

Collect edible roots and shoots in spring when tender, harvest the entire plant in July or when flowers bloom (and dry for later herb use), and gather seed in fall. The root is small and spindle shaped, whitish, slender, and hard (tender when young), but soon gets tough, with a strong aromatic smell.

lacy white tufts of blooms. After flowering, clusters of Queen Anne's lace curl up into nestlike shapes and are picturesque additions to dried flower arrangements.

Salsify

26

Salsify

Tragopogon Porrifolius

*T*hough fashioned like a large aster, salsify has extra-long sepals behind its numerous purple petals, creating a starlike appearance. In addition, its tall stalk usually stands above the wild grasses that surround it. But unless it is morning, most people miss this wildflower. An early bloomer, it closes at around noon and forms a tight bud that blends in with the neighboring grasses.

Immigrants from Eurasia and Africa brought salsify to America. For two thousand years they and their ancestors had cultivated it and eaten the roots. They compared the taste to oysters or artichokes. Once in the New World, the domestic flowers "escaped" and turned wild. Native Americans discovered the plant and immediately put it to use. Besides eating it, they chewed the stems, letting its milky sap help remedy indigestion.

My Wonderings . . .

> In those days John the Baptist came preaching in the wilderness. . . . John himself was clothed in camel's hair, with a leather belt around his waist; and his food was locusts and wild honey.
>
> Matthew 3:1–4 NKJV

John the Baptist started out as the son of a respected, "domesticated" priest and his devout wife. He ended up living in the wilderness, wearing camel skins, and eating locusts. Somehow God has a way of adding an unpredictable side to our lives.

Personally, I like tame living. No one would ever accuse me of having a wild streak. But every so often God edges me beyond my preferred domestic comfort. I can look back just a couple of years and remember when I lived a quiet widow's life, walking my dog, teaching college, and enjoying moved-out, grown children. Today, I'm married to a pastor, have five stepchildren (two still at home), and struggle to even find time for a walk.

I hadn't planned on heading down a new tangled path of overwhelming love, church shepherding, stepparenting, and busyness. But I wouldn't change a thing. As a widow, I felt my comfort zone getting smaller and smaller. But not today. Now I'm amazed at what I'm willing to do.

God knows when domesticity needs a little wilderness.

Your Wanderings . . .

Late April through September, you'll find salsify's purple or yellow flowers in sunny meadows and along roads or railroad tracks—that is, if you're an early bird. Blooms typically close at the sun's peak in the day.

Sweet and Salsified

To enjoy common salsify beyond its bloom in the field, wait for it to form a seed head.

In bouquets: The large, fluffy, dandelion-type puffs can be carefully picked and sprayed with a thin lacquer to preserve for dry bouquets.

For the dining table: Harvest salsify's edible root, which is also known as the vegetable oyster, to use in soups and stews (boil and cream it like you would asparagus), or boil and mash it to eat like a potato, or cut it into long strips like French fries to sauté in butter for a snack. You can enjoy the roots all winter by covering salsify plants in your garden with straw or leaf mulch in the fall. Shoots that start in winter give salads a nice flavor.

27

Scotch Broom

Cytisus Scoparius

*A*n abundance of brilliant yellow, pealike blossoms decorate this wild shrub. Thinking the colorful bush would add to his property, a Scots captain named Colquhoun Grant brought it to Victoria, Canada, in 1849. Only three of the plants survived, but it was enough. They have populated the entire western side of the hemisphere.

Though Scotch broom is now considered troublesome because of this "takeover" persistence, folklore tells how early pioneers found "broom" handy when their coffee ran out. After blooming, this shrub produces seed-filled pods that dry naturally on its branches. When brushed by man or beast, the seeds rattle in the pods. Clued by this distinct noise, settlers found, roasted, and brewed the dark beans for a hot drink. When not harvested, the pods burst and fling their seeds many feet.

However, modern wild crafters (those who harvest wild foliage) warn that Scotch broom contains toxic alkaloids that can depress the hearing and nervous systems, and it should not be consumed in any form.

My Wonderings . . .

In the same way, let your light shine before men, that they may see your good deeds and praise your Father in heaven.

Matthew 5:16

A delicate lace cross hangs in my front door window. On a living room wall, rough-cut brass letters that spell JESUS dangle from connecting brass rings. I like these things in my home to remind me of the Lord. I also like to share with others what's important in my life. But sometimes I think I also want to make sure visitors know Jesus Christ is vital to me. I guess I don't quite trust that I live well enough for it to be seen.

Funny, Scotch broom doesn't worry about rattling loud enough or flinging its seeds far enough. Yet it doesn't have any problems multiplying.

I think I make sharing Jesus Christ with others a lot harder than God intended it to be. I worry about the response of others, but I can't control it. I carry mistakes when I've asked for forgiveness. I tackle inner issues from the outside. My fretfulness doesn't improve my ability to tell others about the Lord. But being who I am does.

Your Wanderings . . .

Found in sunny, open areas, Scotch broom can spend two to four years in a grasslike state until it establishes an extensive root system and flourishes with pea-shaped flowers grouped in clusters on stems. Look for the light yellow to orange or

Scotch broom's deep green leaves and waxy stems remain a popular accent to floral decorations, but you can enjoy the wild side of these plants by listening to them "sing" in the field. Listen for the rattle of Scotch broom seed pods when they're touched or moved by the wind.

You may even hear a crack and pinging of a dozen scattering seeds. The hard-shelled, pealike pod is covered with fine, soft hairs; when the pod dries at maturity, the two halves warp in different directions, eventually opening and snapping as seeds are cast four to twelve feet away.

crimson to purple blooms in summer's prime, June through August. You'll find many a florist looking for harvest yields of Scotch broom September through May, when it's dormant and quality can be maintained during storage, processing, and shipment for floral arrangements.

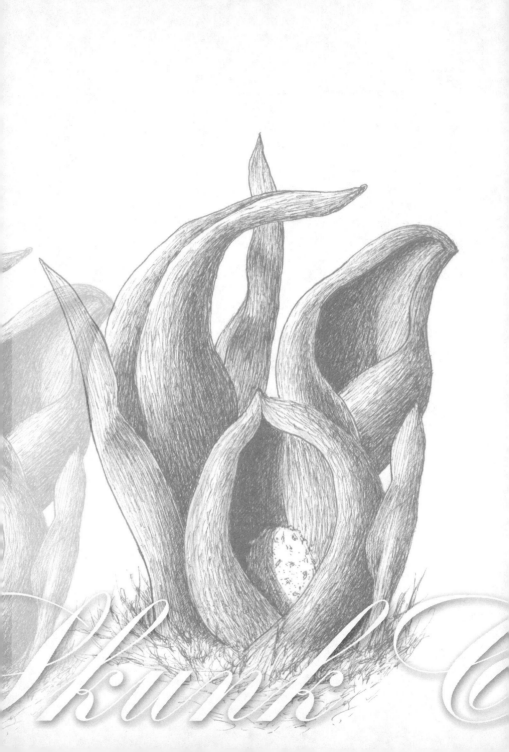

28
Skunk Cabbage
Lysichitum Americanum

*A*t first glance skunk cabbage looks like a single tropi-
cal flower stuck in the mud. But the large yellow
cape that swathes the thick center spike is not a petal. It acts
more like a sepal, protecting dozens of small green flowers as
they develop on the club-shaped spike. After unfurling and
turning yellow, the cape backdrops the club's flowered head.
Large, broad leaves, some up to fifty-six inches long, grow
around the cape and club.

Settlers used the sap from this bloom to treat ringworm.
Native Americans, however, made it the object of tribal legends and a food source when starvation threatened. But its
most practical use came from the leaves. Much like a mom
today would grab a paper towel, Native Americans used skunk
cabbage's large leaves to cover food, line berry baskets, and
provide a clean surface for preparing meals. Bears, meanwhile,
dined on the fleshy stems of skunk cabbage for a wake-up
meal.

My Wonderings . . .

My soul shall be joyful in my God;
For He has clothed me with the garments of salvation,
He has covered me with the robe of righteousness.

Isaiah 61:10 NKJV

I can appreciate the resourcefulness of Native American women using skunk cabbage leaves like paper towels, but I struggle with where they got them. The idea of slogging through black, foot-sucking mud to get food covers and basket liners triggers an inner yuck that stream water can't quite wash away. Having seen skunk cabbages growing in the wild, I can imagine the trek—gooey sludge squishing between my toes and oozing up my ankles while a zillion tiny creatures of the mud world touch me. No paper towel would be worth it.

But the truth is, that is exactly what Jesus Christ did when he left his perfect heaven to claim his people in a sinful world. He trekked through adulterous women, thieving tax collectors, disease-ridden outcasts, brutal Roman soldiers, and dozens of other disgusting undesirables—including me.

Looking back and seeing how he plucked me from the muck, cleaned me, and covered me with his robe of righteousness, I feel amazed. How God must love me!

Your Wanderings . . .

This unique wildflower can brighten bogs as early as February. Yet flowers bloom more frequently in April and May in stream beds, wet banks, marshlands, and moist woods—often among cattails. The blooms appear as tiny spikes, especially compared to the plant's clusters of giant leaves and tall stalks.

Just Say "Freeze!"

Capture a skunk cabbage on film in winter and you'll discover a whole new dimension to this flower's beauty. Often winter isn't finished when this plant blooms, and sparkling snow or frost can dust its yellow cape, flower-covered club, and long leaves, creating unusual and striking pictures. Best of all, the mud typically surrounding skunk cabbage is frozen—so you don't have to ooze through it for the shot.

29

Teasel

Dipsacus Sylvestris

easel produces an oval head on its stout stem. Dozens of small bluish lavender flowers cover the rounded dome. Short spikes nestle in and around the blooms, looking a bit like a floral porcupine. In addition, thorns cover the plant's stem and leaves.

This thistle hails from Europe and loves open lands with full sun. After the teasel's small flowers wither away, florists and crafters use the dried spiked heads in bouquets and projects. They often spray them with metallic paint, creating unusual bursts of sparkle.

But long before modern artisans clipped the teasel heads, woolen mill workers did the same. They used the prickly pods to comb the tangles, snarls, and debris out of sheared lamb fleece. Only then was the wool spun into thread for fabric.

My Wonderings . . .

No discipline seems pleasant at the time, but painful. Later on, however, it produces a harvest of righteousness and peace for those who have been trained by it.

Hebrews 12:11

Hard times and I know each other well. I lost my first husband to cancer when I was only thirty-four years old. I raised four children alone and watched one choose to walk away from God. Each of these tough situations gouged my heart. The pain made me feel like I couldn't breathe. The myriad of tears made my eyes hurt and my head ache. I felt sure I couldn't go on.

But somehow I did. A Bible verse, a friend, the words of a song—something would allow me to see God, not as I'd seen him before, but in a clearer way, a deeper way. The new glimpse of my Lord would stem my tears and help me take a breath.

I never want to repeat any of my hard times. They hurt too much. But I also would not want to be who I was before they struck my life. Somehow they "combed" the tangles and debris out of me. Somehow they made me a better person.

Sharpening Decor

Often called "gypsy combs" and grown commercially as nature's lint brush, teasel blooms can be dried for beautiful flower arrangements and wreaths.

For a lovely Christmas wreath, purchase a Styrofoam wreath from a craft department or shop. Wearing good, protective gloves, cut off two or three dozen dried teasel heads with an inch of the stem. Push the stems into the Styrofoam until the prickly pods cover it.

Leave the wreath natural or spray paint it a desired color. Add a bow or other dried plant pieces as a finishing touch.

Your Wanderings . . .

Late summer through October, look in prairies, savannas, seeps, and sedge meadows, along roadsides, and even near dumps to find the whitish blooms on cut-leaved teasel and lavender blooms on the common plant. The leaves appear to form cups and may even hold water. Flowers are small and packed on dense, oval-shaped heads.

30

Tiger Lily

Lilium Columbianum

*L*ike most members of its family, the tiger lily strikes viewers with its beauty. Maroon spots dot its rich orange petals, giving them the look of tiger fur. Each bloom hangs downward from arched branches off a main stem. Though facing the ground, the flower's six elongated petals curl upward, revealing its bold colors, vase-shaped pistil, and anther-tipped[13] stamens.

Tiger lilies grow in open forests during May through August and can reach up to four feet in height. Though some Native American tribes ate lily bulbs, this family of flowers filled more legends than dinner plates. One English folk-belief contended that anyone who smelled a tiger lily would end up with freckles.

My Wonderings . . .

And why do you worry about clothes? See how the lilies of the field grow. They do not labor or spin. Yet I tell you that not even Solomon in all his splendor was dressed like one of these.

Matthew 6:28–29

For twenty-five years wildflowers captured my attention and sent me on a quest to learn about them. As I explored my own properties, hiked mountain trails, and walked beside rivers, never once did I exclaim, "Look at how fat that flower is!" or "How can that plant stand being so tall?"

My nonquestioning attitude doesn't stop with flowers. I've never queried God about his unique creativity of shells, birds, or even creepy insects. Yet for some reason, I tend to cross-examine him regarding his creation job on me. As a teen, I wanted thick, long hair. As a young mom, I wanted a shape that bounced right back to its pre-pregnancy size. As a maturing woman, I wanted to skip menopause. It seems like the mirror and the way God created me always clash.

Maybe it's time I considered the lilies. Should I be made just right for a mirror or just right for the Lord's purposes? If I feel awed by his handiwork in a tiger lily, should I not be awed by his handiwork in me?

Wild Thing

Domestic and wild lilies, with bell-shaped blooms that often hang like pendants or in starbursts from their stems, make gorgeous bouquets.

Freshness can be prolonged by cutting each stem diagonally before placing it in a vase or floral foam. Also, add to the water a small amount of ammonium chloride, potassium nitrate, sodium carbonate, or camphor to retard germ growth.

Your Wanderings . . .

Growing in prairies, thickets, and lower-altitude mountain forests, the tiger lily's showy blooms of orange-red with purple spots can be found in June and July. Find them before any resident deer do, as the blooms are a favorite snack.

In fact, many Native Americans in the Pacific Northwest also enjoyed dining on tiger lilies—steaming or boiling the blooms and often the bulbs, and sometimes drying them for future use.

31

Trillium

Trillium Ovatum

rillium's early appearance each spring earned it a second common name—"wake-robin." Eastern Native American tribes also called it "birthroot," because they used it as a relaxant and pain reliever during childbirth. Past tribesmen, as well as modern-day hikers, easily spotted the flower. Its creamy white and lush green colors stand a foot above the dark, wet, decaying ground cover left by winter.

A closer look gives even more appreciation for the flower's conspicuousness. It is a perfect symmetry of threes. Three matched white ovate petals unfold above three narrow sepals that fill the spaces between each petal. And on the stem below, a swirl of three evenly spaced leaves continues the pattern. Nothing about the trillium's tri-design looks random or uneven.

My Wonderings . . .

Go and make disciples of all the nations, baptizing them in the name of the Father and of the Son and of the Holy Spirit.

Matthew 28:19

Sets of threes surround me. My breakfast egg has a yolk, a white, and a shell. The tree outside my window has roots, a trunk, and leaves. And even I have a body, soul, and spirit. Yet I struggle to grasp the Bible's reference to a single almighty God who has three "persons"—the Son Jesus Christ, the Holy Spirit, and God the Father.

Over the years, I've handled my confusion in a variety of ways. I've tried to explain it, using the egg example. I've tried to avoid it, hoping no one would bring it up. And I've tried to bluff past it, arguing the meaning of Bible verses.

Why do I need to figure God out? It's not like I'm in his league. He's infinite; I'm finite. He's all knowing; I'm a mere college graduate. He's unlimited by restraints; I'm stuck in a body. Realizing our vast differences allows me to come to terms with his one-in-three description. Understanding God's goodness is beyond me, but knowing him personally is just a prayer away.

Your Wanderings . . .

Trillium appears in spring with the first robins returning from winter. Blooming March through June, the grand, three-petaled flowers pop from lush green forestlands and shady mountain woodlands.

Though tricky, and though requiring certain permissions for this protected wildflower, you can transplant trilliums[14] and watch them bloom year after year.

Take only mature plants that have bloomed, since from seeds trillium can take four years to flower. Look closely inside a flower with a hand lens and count their three stigmas but be careful not to trample them or the soil where they grow. Carefully dig at least eight inches around the plant's base to keep the underground bulb and surrounding soil intact, as trillium's sugars are stored in the rhizomes or roots.

Trilliums prefer shady, damp forest floor soils that are rich in nitrogen, but they will grow at low to middle elevations in partially shaded areas with low- to mid-light levels. They like a soil rich in deciduous leaf mulch such as maple or birch. If the soil is less than ideal and your trilliums look stunted, give them a fall and spring bonemeal application.

32
Twinflower
Linnaea Borealis

A thin-branched stem rises from twinflower's base of shiny emerald leaves. At the end of each branch, a delicate pink bell looks ready to ring at the slightest breeze. But it isn't sound that fills the air; it's a sweet fragrance.

This aromatic quality made twinflower a favorite of the early botanist Carolus Linnaeus, who developed our present system of scientifically identifying plants with two names, one generic and one specific. His idea of "twin" names probably didn't come from this plant, but his delight in it led others to name it after him.

Though originally identified in Lapland (Scandinavia) in 1737, twinflower is found today in shaded forests from northern Europe, around the North Pole, and down into China, Russia, Greenland, Canada, and the United States.

My Wonderings . . .

Two are better than one,
    because they have a good return for their work:
If one falls down,
    his friend can help him up.
But pity the man who falls
    and has no one to help him up!
Also, if two lie down together, they will keep warm.
    But how can one keep warm alone?
Though one may be overpowered,
    two can defend themselves.
A cord of three strands is not quickly broken.

Ecclesiastes 4:9–12

As a married woman, I knew the truth of these verses. But as a single woman and mother, I often felt mocked by them. Some helpful friends suggested I take a spiritual view, seeing God as the other half of my duo. But I knew Solomon meant just what he wrote—two literal bodies to help work, support, warm, and defend each other.

So where did that leave me, a descendant of many "pull yourself up by your bootstraps" Americans? It left me trying to do things myself. But one day, after I'd spent hours breaking off pieces of a faulty tub faucet, a neighbor told me about a little hidden screw that would have allowed me to pull it off in a minute. That's when I realized God had me in a school of "other" dependence.

I didn't want to be there, but after a few more fiascoes, I started listening when his Holy Spirit whispered, "Ask Don to cut down your tree" and "Ask Stan to take your trash when he goes to the dump." And then God pushed even more. "Ask

For ground cover in a shaded area, a gardener can't go wrong with twinflower. Root runners make it transplantable, and wherever sunshine dapples its rich green leaves, a stem will rise up and display two matched fragrant blossoms.

For those who love to scrapbook family photographs, pressed twinflowers make a great symbolic decoration for pages commemorating best friends, a wedding, sisters, or other duos. Backdrop the flowers with acid-free paper. Be sure the blooms do not touch any photos.

Frank and Naomi over for Thanksgiving." "Ask Ellen to pray with you."

I did. Two heads are better than one.

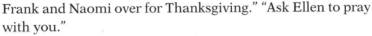

Your Wanderings . . .

Look in moist, shady places June through early August for these pink or white blooms that hang "upside down" in pairs among creeping shiny leaves. Your nose, however, may first find the sweet, fragrant scent released by the sun, as the twinflower is part of the honeysuckle family.

33
Wild Blackberry
Rubus Laciniatus (or Vitifolius)

The delicate white petals of the blackberry blossoms look like they need to be ironed. In the center of the five "wrinkled" petals stands a cluster of fine stamens. These will eventually turn into tangy sweet berries that vary in color from red to black. After the blooms and fruit, the plant's delicacy and sweetness disappear amid a tangle of spiked vines and leaves.

Blackberry plants need little encouragement to grow. They produce seed with or without pollination, and even their vines, when covered with dirt, can produce roots. They tend to take over areas, developing brambles that can rival the size of a house. But Native Americans and early pioneers endured the pokes and scratches from the thorny thickets in order to reach the plant's tasty berries.

My Wonderings . . .

Let us fix our eyes on Jesus, the author and perfecter of our faith, who for the joy set before him endured the cross, scorning its shame, and sat down at the right hand of the throne of God.

Hebrews 12:2

For years this verse from Hebrews made little sense. Jesus experienced such dark hours of deep suffering before and on the cross. How could he equate joy with its spiked crown and blood-covered beams? I found my answer in a blackberry patch.

When I lived in the country, I let a tangle of blackberries take over the bottom of my two acres. Every summer, I donned jeans and a long-sleeve shirt, got some clippers, and headed for the massive thicket.

As I cut paths into the heart of the labyrinth, the spiked tentacles grabbed at my clothes and hair, piercing and scratching me dozens of times. So why did I do it?

For the results—buckets of juicy berries. Nothing compares to the savory taste of warm blackberry pie with vanilla ice cream or the sweet smell of hot, thickened blackberries piled on pancakes.

Jesus's joy was not in the cross's crown of thorns or its rough wood. It was in its results—the salvation of his people.

Your Wanderings . . .

Look in grassy fields or hillsides, vacant lots, coastal scrubland, freshwater marshlands, and riparian woods for the white to pink clusters of wild blackberry flowers in June. By July, sweet, black aggregates of berries form in drupelets.

Wild and Wonderful

If you live by or visit an area with wild blackberries, make an effort to pick some to bring sweet, unique flavor to all kinds of food: muffins, pies, even salads.

A simple ice cream or pancake topping can be made by combining in a microwavable bowl:

1 quart of fresh blackberries
1 to 1½ cups sugar (depending on the berries' tartness)
2 to 3 tablespoons cornstarch
½ teaspoon grated lemon rind

Microwave on high for three minutes, stir, and microwave again. Repeat until bubbly and thick—and enjoy.

34

Wild Flax

Linum Perenne

*T*he five rounded petals of a flax bloom open flat, revealing a delicate blue color offset by a yellow center. A
slender stem hugged by a few short, narrow leaves supports each
one-inch flower. This dainty bloom grows on dry prairie flats
and subalpine ridges, and even slight breezes make it quiver.

Contrary to its wild, frail looks, flax is a commercial giant
that has been cultivated for thousands of years—both linen
and linseed oil come from it. Flax has been an important
source of fiber and oil since prehistoric times, as evidenced
by remnants of fine linen found in Swiss lake dwellings and
in ancient Egyptian tombs.

The value of flax is not limited to ancient times. In the
wild it proved valuable to several Native American tribes
that used it to make cordage. And today, it is a multimillion-
dollar industry.

My Wonderings . . .

Therefore I take pleasure in infirmities, in reproaches, in needs, in persecutions, in distresses, for Christ's sake. For when I am weak, then I am strong.

2 Corinthians 12:10 NKJV

No one would ever mistake me for an athlete. I've always battled a few extra pounds and have never excelled in any sport. But neither have I experienced long-term illness or disability. So for the last twenty years, I've swum and walked regularly.

But this year, I suddenly found myself on a "take for life" medication, and I often fight for energy. An unforeseen risk factor now nags my exercise routine. Will I feel okay or wiped out when I'm done?

I hate feeling frail. I want to go back to just being me.

But as I've remembered and written about the wispy, thin wild flax I identified on a dry slope years ago, my thoughts have edged away from what I've lost to a potential gain. In my unwanted frailness, will God find a new avenue for his strength? Will he transform my weakness into something useful and good? He did it for this wildflower. Am I not worth more than a flower, "which is here today and tomorrow is thrown into the fire" (Matt. 6:30)?

Your Wanderings . . .

Look for the white, blue, or purple flowers of wild flax (there are several types) creating a colorful wave on earthy banks and gravelly slopes in July and August. Many gardeners use flax, which has flowery blooms that appear delicate and frail, because it's strong and grows readily in many soils.

Seeds for Body and Soul

A variety of flax seeds and young plants can be purchased from nurseries, seed catalogues, and online sites. Some are grown for garden use, while others are grown to be eaten like sprouts. To grow them for your own use, follow these simple directions.

1. Pick a spot in full sun, or in hot climates, in part shade. Make sure the soil drains well, because flax does not like soggy ground.
2. Place plants six inches apart.
3. Put a small amount of organic fertilizer into each planting hole.
4. Mulch around, not on, plants with organic compost.
5. Water until soil is completely moist.
6. After the flax flowers, cut back plants to within three or four inches from the ground.

35

Woolly Mullein

Verbascum Thapsus

Woolly mullein's tall spiral of bright yellow flowers has decorated dry roadsides since its creation. But its stately beauty does much more than adorn stark terrain. For thousands of years people have found uses for its leaves, flowers, and stalks.

Quaker girls used its woolly leaves to color their cheeks without the aid of cosmetics, unaware that tiny barbs were actually scratching them. Native Americans dried and smoked mullein to ease lung troubles. Ancient Europeans used it to bleach hair, kill pain, and cure coughs.

But mullein's uses go back even farther to the days of Christ. Romans dipped dry stalks of mullein into tallow and fired them for torches. It may well be that the soldiers who arrested Jesus in the Garden of Gethsemane used this dried flower to light their way.

My Wonderings . . .

When Jesus spoke again to the people, he said, "I am the light of the world. Whoever follows me will never walk in darkness, but will have the light of life."

John 8:12

I know darkness. For fourteen years I lived in a mountain home surrounded by towering fir trees. No sunlight ever glistened through my front bay window. At the time, I did not mind.

Then I needed to move. House after house, I searched for the right size, color, and shape. One step into any shaded room, and I'd shake my head no. Unknown to me, the years of darkness had left me starved for light. I agreed to buy only where sunbeams spilled through windows.

Later I came to see this as an illustration of life. We can live with darkness and be happy. But once we've experienced light, darkness is always . . . dark, not so pleasant as light, and sometimes much worse—lonely, scary, overwhelming. In the same way, we can live without Jesus Christ and be happy. But if we experience him, if we come to know the light of the world, he somehow becomes essential. We need him. He alone lights our darkness.

Your Wanderings . . .

Look for woolly mullein to appeal to your sense of touch as well as sight with its soft, velvety, downy leaves on woody stems throughout summer. It's found mostly on sun-washed, stony ground, by roadsides, and in woodland clearings.

Out of the garden, mullein can come to your aid in a variety of ways:

Breathe in an infusion to ease coldlike symptoms. Let the plant dry, then crumble leaves, the bloom, and the stem into your vaporizer's water. The resulting steam should ease your symptoms.

Make an aromatic tea. Boil one tablespoon dried mullein leaf or root to each cup of water for five to ten minutes. Be sure to strain out the plant's woolly hairs, because they can irritate throat tissues. A sweetener can be made by infusing the fresh or dried flowers. For a creamier treat, use milk instead of water for boiling.

Make an essential oil purported to help lower blood pressure. Place one cup of mixed mullein flowers, seed, and root in a blender to crush and mince. Fill a small jar with the mix that's then doused with olive oil. Cover the jar and set it in a warm place for two weeks. Strain before using.

Yarrow

36

Yarrow

Achillea Millefolium

*T*iny, daisylike flowers form yarrow's creamy round umbel head, and fine hairs cover the stalk and fern-style leaves. The entire plant produces a pungent herbal smell, especially when picked. It reproduces by roots and seeds.

From ancient times to present day, people have used yarrow for medical purposes. Ancient Greeks, medieval knights, and American Civil War soldiers made it into a salve to help stop bleeding; others drank it as a tea to relieve melancholy and colds. These uses led people to give yarrow a variety of other names, including "soldier's woundwort," "nose bleed," and "stanch weed." Even today, herbalists endorse its healing qualities.[15]

My Wonderings . . .

He said to them, "Why are you troubled, and why do doubts rise in your minds? Look at my hands and my feet. It is I myself! Touch me and see."

Luke 24:38–39

Several small white lines and patches from a lifetime of cuts and scrapes scar my arms and legs. Yet for many years, I never associated scars with God's healing. Somehow, I thought his divine touch made heart and soul wounds disappear.

One day, the marks on Jesus's hands and feet confronted this belief. The torn holes made by the cross nails were healed, but they left behind visible scars.

Looking back on my own life, I realized I too have inner scars from God-healed wounds. I no longer wince in pain when I speak of them, but they always produce an internal pause. And at times, a word, a song, or a sight can trigger their full memory.

Somehow these leftover reminders of God's restoring touch become something good—comfort for another person, or a helpful action, or a heartfelt prayer of empathy. As with the scars on Jesus's hands and feet, God left my inner scars for a purpose.

Your Wanderings . . .

Look for the white (and occasionally pink) flowering yarrow June through September in sunny, grassy areas and old fields; along fence lines, roadsides, and other edges; and sometimes in lawns.

With an ancient and honorable reputation as a "wound herb" that can stop the flow of blood, yarrow has long been heralded for its healing properties.

Even while in the garden it can work benefits. Yarrow attracts beneficial syrphid flies (also called "flower flies" or "hover flies"). These are bright yellow or black and orange flies that resemble yellow jackets or wasps but are harmless to humans and in the larval stage consume huge quantities of garden-harmful insects like aphids. Syrphid flies are important because they feed early in the season when it may be too cool for other beneficial insects. Yarrow also acts as an activator to speed the decomposition of compost. To see results, you only need one finely chopped leaf per wheelbarrow load of compost material.

Beauty beyond the garden: Yarrow makes attractive dried flowers. To dry, cut blooms at their peak, before they start to fade and bleach in the sun. Hang six to twelve flowers in clusters or bouquets, head-down, in a dry, airy place out of the sun. Flowers can take at least a week to dry and then can be used in arrangements or as a fragrant addition to potpourri.

As edibles in the kitchen: Yarrow leaves can be used as a seasoning, somewhat like sage (the flowers add an even stronger flavor). Young leaves have been boiled as greens like spinach, and very young, fresh leaves can be added to salads.

As a soothing skin and beauty treatment: Make a simple yarrow and chamomile lotion by combining one tablespoon dried yarrow flowers and foliage and one tablespoon dried chamomile flowers in a bowl. Add two cups boiling water. Leave in a warm place for thirty minutes. Stir again, then strain off the liquid. Pour into glass bottles and store in the refrigerator.

Notes on Flowery Language

1. **Scientific Name:** Unlike the common names of wildflowers, the scientific ones are precise, differentiating between one kind of flower's many close relatives. Often only a botanist can sort through all the dandelions, lupines, blackberries, and other family varieties. As a result, a plant in your area that looks like one in this book might have a slightly different scientific name.

2. **Sepals:** Sepals are the green leaflike sheath that covers a flower's bud. When the flower opens, the sepals usually fold back and remain beneath the bloom.

3. **Medicine and Food Uses:** Though wildflowers have been used for medicine, drinks, and food for centuries, this book does not provide enough information for a reader to try the uses given. The few exceptions in the "Your Wanderings" sections are well-known with little or no risk.

4. **Picking Plants:** It's illegal to pick or uproot plants in national, state, and local parks, forests, and wildernesses. Outside of these lands, many wildflowers can be picked, but most states stipulate that it must be at least fifty feet off a road. If in doubt about picking a plant, check with your local forest or park service.

5. **Tuber:** This looks like the beginning of a plant's root system, but it is actually an underground stem that stores food.

6. **Wild and Domestic Flowers:** Many wildflowers have been domesticated, and some domesticated ones have escaped into the wild. Though the two share similar structures, it is usually easy to tell them apart. Domesticated flowers are almost always larger and can be purchased in a much wider variety of colors.

7. **Stamen:** Stamens are filaments usually located at the center of a bloom. They are tipped with anthers, often giving the appearance of skinny little legs wearing oversized shoes.

8. **Raceme:** This is one of many words that denote a plant's flowering pattern. A raceme refers to a main stalk that has many flowers blooming along it, such as with foxglove.

9. **Pistil:** This "female" part of a flower is usually located at the bloom's center. Though not visible on all plants, it often resembles a long-neck vase. It is essential to pollination and the plant's reproduction.

10. **Rhizome:** For the general onlooker, a rhizome is just a root. But unlike a normal root, this one has "nodes" that store food and can produce a new plant.

11. **Creeper:** Though this sometimes refers to any prostrate plant that grows along the ground, it specifically refers to a plant that produces trailing shoots that can take root at its nodes or "joints."

12. **Umbel:** Like *raceme*, this word describes a plant's flowering pattern. An umbel refers to umbrella-like clusters of smaller flowers that form what appears to be a single large, round bloom. Queen Anne's lace is an umbel.

13. **Anther:** This is the sacklike part of a stamen that contains the pollen. It is usually located on the stamen's outer tip. Anthers can look like oversized shoes on stamen "legs."

14. **Trillium:** This wildflower is endangered today. If the flower is picked, the plant rarely blooms again, stopping the plant's ability to reproduce.

15. **Herbalist:** A person who sells medical herbs. He or she is usually knowledgeable about the healing benefits of wild and domestic plants. The recent trend toward natural medicine has increased the number of herbalists.

Field Guides
Favorite Reading for Walks in the Meadow

The Audubon Society Field Guide to North American Wildflowers (Western Region) by Richard Spellenberg (New York: Knopf, 1988). This was my first wildflower book, and its easy color key made it great for a beginner. It is reprinted and updated regularly and can be found in most bookstores.

Wild Flowers of the Pacific Northwest by Lewis J. Clark (Sidney, BC: Gray's Pub., 1976). Though out of print, this wonderful book can be found through online and used book retailers. It has full-color plates and good flower histories.

A Field Guide to Pacific States Wildflowers by Theodore F. Niehaus (Boston: Houghton Mifflin, 1976). This guidebook is regularly updated and reprinted for different regions throughout the United States. It is specific to flower identification with no histories or uses. But when I'm stuck and can't identify a flower, this book usually helps me find it.

Familiar Friends by Rhoda Whittlesey (Oregon: Rose Press, 1985). I found this book in a used bookstore, and undoubtedly copies can be found online. Though lacking in good drawings or color plates, the book contains excellent flower histories and ideas on uses.

Wildflowers of Kentucky by Nevyle Shackelford (University of Kentucky). This locally published, black-and-white, staple-bound book provided some interesting information that did not appear in other books. I also have these types of books from Yosemite National Park, the San Juan Islands, and other places. If you travel, look for these local wildflower information books/pamphlets published by universities, national parks, and local organizations.

Common Edible and Useful Plants of the East and Midwest by Muriel Sweet (Healdsburg, CA: Naturegraph Publishers, 1975). These black-and-white books on edible plants feature helpful line drawings. They are more practical than historical but do contain some interesting information.

Index

About the Author

Deborah Hedstrom-Page is a speaker, writer, and pastor's wife who lives in Jasper, Oregon. She speaks regularly at women's retreats and meetings, and frequently teaches writing in college classes and workshops. She's the former writer-in-residence at Western Bible College in Salem, Oregon; the author of ten junior-age American history books; and coauthor of a devotional for caregivers. Her articles have appeared in more than three hundred publications, and she wrote a single mothering column in *Home Life* magazine based on the fifteen years she lived as a widow raising four children on her own. She recently married a pastor and loves her new life. In addition to her four children, she has five stepchildren and four grandkids, all of whom she loves to introduce to the wildflowers on her two-acre home out in the country.

About the Illustrator

Kevin Ingram, a professional illustrator and graphic artist in Grand Rapids, Michigan, works in a wide range of media, from oil to computer-aided design. He specializes in portraiture and freelance work for the publishing industry.

As he began research on the wildflowers to illustrate for this book, he thought of domesticated plants versus ones he saw on a hiking trek in the Adirondacks of northern New York State. That's where he came across a patch of Indian Pipe, high in the mountains. The flowers clung to a rock face with a southern exposure. With not even acceptable light for most plants, the spot seemed a strange place for a flower garden. He was struck by how this white, scaly flower—not the most beautiful of blooms—had an impressive ability to thrive in an inhospitable environment.

"There is a wildness to this world of flora," he observed. "These plants are not pampered with laboratory-tested fertilizer or bedded with several inches of weed-free elbow-room. Instead, these flowers thrive in untamed wilderness, where unexpected beauty peeks from mountainsides and where the planting and tending is done by God's artistic hands. I thought how Jesus encouraged us to trust by the lilies of the field (Matt. 6:28–30), how sometimes we are called to live out that trust on a cliff where God's planted us. It may be a strange place for a garden and uncomfortable, but God roots his people in him. We may look untamed, unkempt, or scruffy, but we're the wildflowers that are planted to persevere in his grace."

When Befriending Flowers . . .

After delving into the design and designer of so many wonderful wildflowers, you may feel an urge to find, to examine, to pick, to take home your newly discovered treasures. But think before you do so.

The national park and forests services state: "Picking wildflowers or collecting specimens of animals, trees, or minerals in all national parks and monuments is prohibited without special permission from the park superintendent. Study the plants where they grow, take home photographs of them, but leave them for the enjoyment of those who will follow."

Many state parks have similar restrictions, and some states even place limits on picking wildflowers on all private and state lands, including roadsides. Be sure you know the laws of your state.

But even without such laws, consider before picking. Only a few wildflowers reproduce by bulbs; most do so by seeds. When you pick the flower's bloom, no seed pod can form to scatter next year's seeds. Besides, even when pressed or preserved, wildflowers fade and lose their beauty. Only in the wild do they look their best.